SNOW CAMPING

© 1974 by
Nordic World Magazine

Library of Congress Catalog No. 74-16796
ISBN 0-89037-0-42-7

Published by

WORLD PUBLICATIONS

Post Office Box 366
Mountain View, Calif. 94040

CONTENTS

Illustrations by Bil Canfield. Photo credits: Dan Johnston (cover, 6, 37), Jack Miller, 74, 86, 101, 110), John O'Shea (12, 34), Fletcher Manley (84).

INTRODUCTION

So you'd like to try snow camping? You'd like to do something exciting, and a little bit dangerous, something to elevate your status among your friends? Well, winter camping could be all that and more. It could also be a disappointing flop or a lethal tragedy—but this will mostly depend on you.

Most people who take up winter camping are backpackers or others familiar and competent in the wilderness. You have perhaps dealt with an off-season snow flurry. And what zealous backpacker has not let his love of the trail urge him into the mountains either too early or too late, while snow still covers the rocks and trails? These experiences may leave you with some idea of what winter camping is like, but don't be fooled.

The main difference between winter and summer camping is in the necessary precision of the winter experience.

In summer, getting good and wet would probably at *worst* be unpleasant. The same situation in winter would be at *best* unpleasant, and if appropriate action isn't taken, could lead to loss of life.

In summer if you run out of stove fuel you can make do with your campfire. The same situation in deep snow can leave you without food and water. Likewise, a wet sleeping bag or torn tent is a summer nuisance but a potential winter disaster. It is really important to be aware of the hazards of winter in such a way as to be able to deal with them effectively. That's partly what this booklet is about.

Equipment is highly important in winter camping and should be chosen with thought and care. Wool is still king for shirts, pants, and socks. It's much more important to have well-made items that are in good condition than newly-made, poor quality, high fashion items. In winter camping your equipment, all of it, has to work well.

How do you do all this? How do you get the knowledge and equipment and, perhaps most important, the attitude to become a winter camper? Reading this booklet and other published literature on the subject will help. But sooner or later, however, you've got to experience the activity. And you must experience it again and again if you want to become proficient at it.

To those just getting started, here are some pointers that may help. Friends can be useful and may even take you along on a trip. But be aware that their zeal for their own favorite piece of gear may prompt them into giving you unreasonable advice. What's just perfect for them may be haphazard for you. This is particularly true about tents. It's wise to first determine what you are likely to be doing—overnight trips? Five-day excursions? And how many people are going to be along—just you and a friend, or are you likely to have a larger party? Consider all of this, take a look at your checkbook and then evaluate the equipment. The salespeople in most mountain specialty shops generally are well informed about the equipment they sell, but they are there, after all, to sell their own brands.

Occasionally a college or recreation department (and sometimes resort areas) will have programs that will help you choose what you need to get properly and easily started. But in the main you are on your own—which isn't so bad: it's probably a more exciting and useful experience that way.

After you've gone through the process of evaluating and selecting all your equipment, I earnestly urge you to do the following: pile all your gear into your car and drive to the place where you'd like to camp. Select a snowy spot 50 yards or so from the car and try the equipment out. *Test everything thoroughly.* Imagine what you would do in a two-day blizzard. Check out your stove. Melt a quart of water and make some soup. Check out the air mattress or foam pad. Practice getting in and out of the tent without filling the interior with snow. Spend the night in your tent and when you awaken in the morning check your energy level. Are your boots dry enough to put on, or are they frozen solid? Did you forget to answer nature's call or were you forced to make a night trip? Can you get your stove started so you can make breakfast?

The beauty of getting started by this "trial-run method" is that even if you flopped on all counts, all you have to do is dash for your car and drive to the nearest restaurant for breakfast. It's far less pleasant to face the realization that if you did everything wrong 10 miles from nowhere you might be the grisly find of a belatedly summoned search party.

To repeat what I said earlier, the main difference between winter and summer camping is in the necessary precision of the winter experience. Nonetheless, thousands of people have become highly competent winter campers. If you go about it properly, you can become one, too.

—LARRY MOITOZO

1 WINTER

THE BEST SEASON

BY JIM HUNTER

Jim Hunter came to Alaska in 1954 courtesy of the U.S. Air Force and, in his own words, he's been "an Arctic bird of sorts ever since." Now living in Fairbanks, he's a year-round outdoorsman, active in everything from kayaking to cross-country skiing. But over the years he's come to prefer winter over the other seasons—as he eloquently explains here.

They say you've really flipped if you like winter better than summer. Well, it was several years and a lot of winters before I realized I was one of those who had slowly drifted over into the lunatic fringe.

Before that, winter camping and cross-country skiing were things you did to kill time while you waited for summer to come again. And Alaskan summers are great. No doubt at all. It's just that one day it dawned on me that the winters are better. And so now everything is reversed.

I do things in the summer, but I am really waiting for the fine moment when things start to freeze up again. I guess the cold gets right in your blood. When it's not cold you don't feel quite right. Without jacket and gloves you feel undressed. And there is a tickle all summer long, a kind of itch you can't quite scratch. On summer trips and at summer gatherings you find yourself daydreaming about the delicious sound of wood cross-countries sliding easily over fresh snow on top of a good packed bottom.

But you don't say too much about that. Your wife prefers Hawaii and sand and burning sun, and so off at the edge of the lawn, summer tonic in hand, even you suspect only a madman could prefer below-zero and short daylight instead of summer's mixed blessings.

But you are hooked and so you quit fighting it and start analyzing it.

"You can't wait until winter gets here!" your friends gasp. "Are you nuts?"

"Listen," you try to explain. "Stop and think about it. The first thing about winter that is downright beautiful is all the tourists go home. Just having the place to ourselves again is great, right?"

"I suppose."

"You can get in the stores for wool socks, for wax, you know what I mean. You can cross the streets in the middle of the block without getting run over."

They nod. Even if they consider you slightly daft they do have to admit that when winter comes the whole land begins to calm. The energetic cycle of birth-life-death that is summer is over. When snow comes the land shrugs and decides to take a rest.

And in the winter stillness the land is somehow more inviting, even more accessible. For its cards are on the table. The ice or cold will kill you if you make a mistake. But unlike summer, which because of its diversity can hold more surprises, winter's traps and pitfalls are more easily avoided by the experienced person.

Trust ice with great fear, dress for and be prepared simply for the worst, and go slowly, very slowly. Learn from an expert and do not blast off blithely into those bright winter woods.

"What else?" they demand.

"Well, the bears are asleep," I tell them happily.

"That is good."

And then I say that summer is overwhelming. There is always a torrent of sensations and events. Things are changing and rushing. Waters roar, birds abound, clouds build to towering heights, forest fires rage, glaciers melt and streams rise, rain pelts, and then there is the constant effort of nearly every living thing preparing hurriedly for the coming winter.

But in winter, without all this fuss going on, one can enter the landscape in a calm frame of mind and for a change enjoy it instead of being completely bowled over by it. As the land sleeps, the outdoorsman moves over it gently and quietly, the snow silencing his movements. He marvels at smaller events which in summer are too easily buried. He stops in a field of windpacked and crusted snow to observe a single, yellow stalk of stiff straw. The yellow flax pokes straight up and around its base the wind has formed a perfect, round pocket. In the pocket the colors of the rainbow are reflected off the many-sided snow crystals.

Above the sky is cloudless and cold blue. Sunrise and sunset come close to each other. The time between when the sky is pink and when it again moves from blue to orange is short. And the yellow sun itself rises and sets in almost the same spot.

After each snowfall the snow is like a fresh blackboard and on it is written what happened the day and night before. The tracks of birds, of shrews and mice, of ermine, fox, rabbits and the marks of the wings of birds of prey tell of every motion which touched earth.

When a fresh fall of snow makes a light cover on the hard surface of a frozen river the tracks of lynx, the great, round paws padding steadily along, are remarkably clear. They indicate a sit-down, a tree-clawing, and a leap over a log. Then the paws meander off into the woods. And the tracks do not run away as the animal would. They can be studied and enjoyed.

When the leaves fall from the trees, the forest is less dense and easier to traverse. The animals with dark coats are easier to see. Moose, caribou, wolves and coyotes stand out against the white.

Wolves use the frozen rivers as they go back and forth in search of food. Their paths become packed and hardened, and their favorite places are well marked.

The winter traveller, whether he is on skis, snowshoes, or using a dog-team, follows and observes the habits of wolves and other predators in a manner impossible in summer.

He cannot see these animals but knows they are there. If they're wolves,

he howls and an answer comes back, and in the still, white, cold world a chilling tingle runs up the base of his neck and down his back, and his shoulders shudder.

In a few minutes the yipping and barking of the whole pack may join in and a howl takes place between human and animal which, in its mutual effort and curiosity, transcends the typical relationship of the two.

Since it is so cold, winter demands less. There is no great push to go roaring off to climb the nearest ridge. For unless you are out specifically to go climbing, the deep snow and chance of freezing will discourage you.

Forced into a tent or cabin you enjoy reading a book or writing up notes of the trip, and afterwards perhaps boiling hot tea and later yet entering a snug sleeping bag. Proper equipment exists to make it all possible, but overcoming the mental barriers is something no catalog can do for you.

The sun does not come busting up at 5 a.m. to ruin a fine morning's snooze and so there is no guilt over sleeping in. But if you are in a wall-tent or cabin, wood must be chopped. And finding wood in winter's snow is much harder than finding it in summer's forest. So you tend to your camp and learn to enjoy it.

A day's cut pile of wood gives as much pleasure as a catch of fine grayling or trout. The stove burning without smoking and the warmth coming from it are small miracles. What you take for granted in the summer you bless in the winter.

If you are in a canvas wall-tent you may have a small Yukon stove. The snow will be covered with caribou robes or spruce limbs and packed flat. A four-inch pipe will poke out the tent roof and inside the temperature will be toasty warm, even if it's 20 below outside.

In your wall-tent you can move around and stand, but in your small, two- or three-man breathing-nylon you will want to be out on the trail or outside.

Winter's restrictions are great, but because you can do less you enjoy more those few things you can do.

You can dress for the cold, but all you can do for summer heat is undress.

But dressed for winter you must move slowly and expect to do less and to concentrate more on just being there. Winter is mellow and summer is not.

Creeping insects, mosquitos, gnats, spiders and other summer creatures have given up the ghost and the winter skier-camper is in a world free of bugs. He does find mosquito larvae in the clear water running beneath the surface of frozen rivers, but he just shakes his head and says to himself, "So that's where the little buggers hide out!"

He finds the woods less crowded and so he does not have to travel great distances to discover solitude (if he can escape or come to terms with snowmachines). And while summer-only people are inside planning, the winter-man is outside doing.

For the winter-man the snow is an annual promise of a trip on a magic carpet. He reaches places summer-only people will never see or know. Swamps impassable in the summer become winter fairy-lands (something Disney could never reproduce) and the swollen, freezing water creates a huge, endless, level platform on which the skier or snowshoer moves through the swamp. Trees and bent brush pop up through the ice. Then the ice mushes up and freezes again, and the winter-man is moved another ten feet above summer-level and moves for miles by tree tops experiencing a world he could not have imagined.

Rivers in summer wall off hidden valleys and mountain passes. In the winter they are gateways and across them the winter-man enters areas untouched in summer.

Winter and winter alone provides the finest outdoor sound one can hear: the sibilant, hushed, wonderful slipping of skis moving well over dry snow. And sometimes this sound comes with a full moon overhead, and in the darkness with the strange moon-shadows, it seems to linger before dissipating into the night air.

And in the gray light the halted winter-man will hear the hissing of owl's wings, the desperate leaping of a snowshoe rabbit, and his own quiet breathing. So in case you've been looking, winter is where it's at.

2
WINTER CAMPING

LESSONS BY BJERKE

BY MEREDITH MOTSON

A *Nordic World* contributor living in Idaho, Meredith Motson wrote this story after participating in a winter-survival course taught by colorful, dynamic wilderness expert Odd Bjerke.

I had seen him around town—a small, plump man with grizzled hair, clumping through the snow with a slight limp. His face was scarred and ruddy, and when he spoke it was with a foreign—perhaps Scandinavian—accent, just different enough to make you wonder who he was and what he was doing in our small mountain town of McCall, Idaho.

Later I was to meet him directly. Due to its heavy snow and subarctic climate, McCall had been chosen as headquarters for a three-day winter survival course, sponsored by the Idaho State Parks and Recreation Department. It was late February—the time of year when work comes to a standstill in McCall, and everyone is looking for some alternative to "cabin fever." Learning to survive seemed a reasonable alternative, and so it was that a varied group of people (myself among them) turned up at the Ponderosa State Park visitor's center early one Thursday morning.

There he was—that same man, looking rather like a rugged Santa who had shaved his beard and donned ski pants and a red sweater for the occasion. He was, he told us, Odd Bjerke (the first name pronounced just as you would hesitate to pronounce it, and the last, *byur-kee*). He would be our instructor for the next three days.

Rather apologetically he began passing out a test. "This is ridiculous... but they want to know how much you learn during the course," he explained.

I glanced down my test :

—"Is perspiration beneficial when hiking in winter?"

—"What percentage of body heat do you lose through your head?"

—"How can you tell which way is up when buried by an avalanche?"

—"Is it more important to have insulation over you or under you?"

I felt a bit sheepish, and to distract myself began to skim another page entitled "A Word About the Program Director": "Mr. Bjerke has spent most of his life in the Arctic and has participated in or led several expeditions to an Arctic environment, such as: 1) Studies in Norwegian Lapland, member of the Jan Mayen expedition, 1942. Received decoration from King Haakon of Norway. 2) Winter survival instructor for the US Air Force. 3) In charge of the main station for the geophysical year expedition to the Greenland Ice Cap. 4) Head of the expedition to the Canadian Arctic, 1967. 5) Head of the San Juan School District Winter Survival and Environmental Program for six years. 6) Head of the Great Slave Expedition of 1972. 7) Head of the Beaufort Expediton, 1971. 8)..."

Then I remembered the test, and, feeling more humble with every page, guessed my way through it.

The test was then collected and shuffled into the office—the last we ever saw of it. Bjerke chuckled, making some comment to the effect that the only thing paper is good for in a survival course "is to make a fire."

"Nature...nature is beautiful," he began, squinting dreamily beyond the walls. "But..." (and his eyes popped open) "Mother Nature does not care about you! She is indifferent! Vinter does not take lives...Man takes lives!"

He cocked his head and grinned, "I mean, ve don't vant to vake up some morning and find ourself in a permanent prone position! So...what ve're basically here for is to learn to live in a snow environment."

Briefly he explained that we would be spending today and tomorrow "in class" and then on Saturday morning we would meet on Brundage Mountain to go through a day of snow-cave building, avalanche training, and emergency techniques, followed by a night of promised warmth deep within our snow caves.

Maybe we didn't believe the part about the warmth. But already there was a genuine emotional warmth in that room for this friend "Odd" who we knew could make a crucial difference in our lives.

"Now I'm going to show you a film I made with my vife, Sam, in the Three Sister Mountains near Bend, Oregon," he announced, switching off the lights. Music swelled through the room as the title flashed across the screen, "Snowcastles." Prior to Odd's own trip, a grim sequence was shown of a young couple lost in the wilderness during a blizzard, and despite the staged quality of their stumbling and fumbling in the knee-deep snow, their final exit from the screen was sobering. They left, stiff and still on stretchers, faces covered.

Then Odd appeared—a younger, thinner version—with his late wife Sam, who "didn't veigh more than 90 pound soaking vet!" Off they set, skiing across the screen, with Odd's sense of humor greatly adding to the narration. They demonstrated how to make snowshoes from limber branches and how to make goggles from bark strips in order to prevent snow blindness. Comments on their equipment, clothing, sleeping gear, how long to travel in a day, how to make camp, build a shelter, and what to eat were included as the sequence progressed. At one point Odd comically "fell" into an ice-capped stream to demonstrate how rolling through dry snow can act like a sponge to dry you off.

Then the lights flashed on again. During one part of the film Odd had demonstrated how one is able to breathe through lightly packed snow, and

The day of the survival trip was brilliantly sunny and Odd Bjerke was the first to begin shedding clothes. Dehydration, he had told the class, is one of the biggest killers in snow country.

now he wanted us to try it. Out into the snow we went, each obediently clapping a handful of snow over mouth and nose. "You can breathe through it because there is thousands of little air pockets per square foot," he instructed. "Now pack it!" Suddenly breathing became impossible.

"Ve vill create an avalanche!" he announced as we went back inside. "Ve vill bury one of you under three and a half to four feet of snow on Saturday—about a ton. That is all that is covering most people who die in avalanches. They die because they panic!"

"Of course, if you see an avalanche coming, the best thing is to try to out-ski it," he continued. "But if you can't make it, then take off your skis and start to breast stroke vith an upvard motion through the snow. If you

Digging a snow cave was a great game and Odd had to get in on the action.

feel yourself being buried, cover your head, vith your arms up, to create an air space. And don't start digging 'til you figure out which vey's up!" I remembered the question on the test. "Spit." "Drop an object." "Watch which way your hand falls" were some of the suggestions from the class. Anything to indicate the direction of gravity.

Odd seemed delighted with the prospect of our man-made avalanche and what a grand time we were going to have burying one of our classmates. And to heighten the hilarity he brought out the park secretary clad in his Eskimo survival suit. Completely lost in the great animal hides, she fumbled to model the various features: the oily wolverine hair around the cuffs and hood (to keep out moisture), the knee-length parka of caribou (because the hair is hollow and holds in warmth), and the sturdy reindeer pants. "In this you can sleep in the snow vith only a pad under you!" Odd claimed. "Anybody vant to wear it Saturday night?"

We all laughed but no one volunteered.

Having touched on the subject of freezing to death, Odd covered the essentials quickly and simply. "If I see a frozen person—I don't care if you are man or voman—I strip you naked and take you into my sleeping bag!"

Warm skin against cold skin, he explained, is the most efficient way to bring heat back into a body that has lost its core temperature. And as for frostbite—"If you see your buddy's nose turning vhite and vaxey, for heaven sake don't rub it! You vill have two noses...one in your hand! Lukevarm vater at about 110 degree is the only safe way to treat it."

There followed a few grisly stories about frostbite victims in our area, topped by worse ones recounted by Odd. Appropriately, he then went through preventative measures, warning that the most susceptible parts of the body are those where the bones come closest to the surface—i.e., fingers, toes, nose and cheekbones. As for the rest of the body, the "layer system" of clothing, properly followed, should greatly reduce risks. To prove it, Odd drew a comical picture of survival clothing from underwear on out, layer after layer, ending with waterproof pants and parka.

Other preventative and emergency techniques followed, from curing diarrhea to amputating a leg—both of which Odd assured us would not be necessary on our trip. One potential accident, though, had to do with a peculiar tendency of human beings when in need of a bathroom outdoors. "For some reason everybody think he got to have a rock or a tree..." Odd mused. "You take a man out in the snow, vith nobody around, and he going to valk a mile 'til he find a rock or tree."

Seeing that we weren't catching on to the potential "danger", Odd told the wry tale of a certain young lady on one of his former survival trips who politely excused herself from the campfire to "gather wood" and simply didn't return. Knowing only too well what had probably happened, Odd finally went in search of a likely tree, and there she was—way down in a hole, in too deep to climb out and too embarrassed to yell. I had forgotten that snow tends to "rot" around trees and boulders, and that you can sink up to your neck or further if you venture too close.

"Don't vorry, though," Odd assured us. "Out of the 36,000 persons I have taken on trips like yours, I only have one accident: a certain physician

Afternoon
left time for
skiing,
picture taking
and checking
the trees in
search of
Norwegian
trolls...

crawls into my snow cave one night and vants me to bandage him but please
not tell anybody. He sat on his own knife."

Informal and humorous, Odd's first lecture had been overwhelming in
its off-hand advice. Techniques far too numerous to mention clogged our
heads as we left for home that day and we were "high" on the prospect of
wilderness living.

The next morning my friend and I skied across frozen Payette Lake to
class (somehow driving to class didn't suit our mood). That day everyone
was to bring their assembled gear for the trip, prepared from a list we had
received earlier. "I vant to check everything that you're going to take up
that mountain," Odd had insisted. So, when we arrived, the room was heaped
with packs, skis, poles and sleeping bags.

First, he had another film to show us, "The Cry of the Loon," starring
none other than himself and Sam again, this time trekking into the no-man's-
land of the Northwest Territories in search of the musk ox. Once again
rugged backpacking, camping and survival techniques were covered; yet,
the major emphasis now turned to the psychology of the explorer. This was
a longer trip—a lonelier trip—much further from the reach of civilization.
Thus, thinking ahead, relying keenly on their own senses, and anticipating
problems before they arose became the key to the success of their venture.
The simple joys of Sam's wild berry pies and Odd's fresh fish, and at last their
encounter with the long-sought herd of musk ox, made it obvious that "one's
state of mind" is *everything* on a wilderness adventure.

Of course, by this time we were eager to be off and doing such things
ourselves, and the fact that we were still sitting in a classroom became tedious.
Yet, Odd had much to cover before the next day and now his instructions
were becoming quite specific.

"Pick a place where the snow has drifted very deep," he advised us about snow caves. First, we were to flatten out a horizontal platform with our skis and then begin tunnelling a short entrance (about a foot and a half) into the snow. From there, he explained, we should begin carving out a domed hollow, allowing only about a foot clearance above the height of an average person sitting up in his sleeping bag, and allowing one half foot to either side of the outermost sleepers. "The dome shape is for strength," he explained. "And don't leave any little tits hanging down or they drip on you!"

"Your body heat will varm the cave from 10 to 20 degree and a single candle vill light it."

Going to bed seemed like a ridiculously elaborate procedure, but Odd insisted that, first, we were to spread out our plastic tarps over the floor of the cave, next our Ensolite (foam) pads, and then our sleeping bags. One by one we were to crawl through the opening, get undressed, and place any extra clothes under our kidney area between the sleeping bag and pad. Boots were to be kept warm under our heads as pillows, and any damp socks could be tossed into the toe of our sleeping bags to dry out overnight. The last person in was to block the cave opening with our packs.

Odd had joked about many things, but about the simple process of going to bed he was very serious. Time and time again he stressed checking over your skin and clothing to make sure everything was dry. "Vipe off any suntan lotion. If you have any moisture on your face it will freeze!" he cautioned.

It seemed that we had been talking about going to bed all morning, yet Odd insisted that these seemingly insignificant details are the ones that, if neglected, cause people to "vake up in a permanent prone position."

Many unsuspecting people also think that a tent and air mattress are perfectly adequate for winter, he added. "But a tent has no insulation and a cold air mattress vill drain you of your body heat!" Again and again he stressed the importance of insulation under the kidney area.

"The quickest way to die if you get stuck in snow country is to sit in your car! If there's no place to tunnel into the snow, then build yourself a lightly packed mound and tunnel in," Odd instructed. "If you have no other insulation, use pine boughs set at an angle to the snow to create dead air space underneath you."

It was noon now and I suppose Odd had realized that we were getting restless because after lunch he started letting us play with things—lighting sterno and heat tape, activating emergency "hot-packs," setting off various smoke signals and emergency flares. We filled the sky with so much orange smoke that afternoon I was surprised that the Forest Service didn't come to our rescue, even though they knew what was going on.

Then it was back inside to recruit an avalanche victim and let him try on Odd's "anti-exposure suit." Bruce Daly, a drummer in a local band, was chosen and amused us all by climbing into the yellow rubber monstrosity of a monkey-suit, complete with feet, hands, hood and a tube-like "elimination hatch."

This over, it was time for Odd to check our gear. "What's this?" he laughed, holding up a paperback book, packed in one woman's equipment. "You know, I read *Lady Chatterley's Lover* six time when I was training troops during the war?...Didn't do no good!"

"And here ve have...". Piece by piece, item by item, he went through our packs, explaining the importance of one item, the ridiculousness of another, and continually amazed at the amounts of food we thought we were going to eat. "People always pack too much food on my trips!" Odd shrugged. "You can go 30 days without food, but only three without water."

He did approve our selection of high protein and high energy foods, however, and read our candy bar labels with great amusement. "And here ve have..." He scrounged for something in the bottom of a pack..."Some dirty long johns!"

So the day ended on a jovial note, though I must admit that we felt a little disdainful about having our packs ransacked. After all, we were adults, and all this prompting seemed a bit much. Our heads were filled with Odd's adventures on the Greenland Ice Cap; his winters training the Tenth Mountain Division of the US Air Force...and our night on Brundage Mountain paled in comparison, especially since it is a ski area.

We agreed, though, to meet there at 10 o'clock the next morning, and to bolster our spirits Odd exclaimed, "After ve have constructed our snow caves, I hope ve have the vorst storm that Idaho have ever experienced!"

We were a varied lot as we gathered under the chairlift the next morning: two Fish and Game officers, a nurse, a school teacher, the drummer, a potter, several Forest Service employees, and several carpenters—sixteen of us in all. Yet in one respect we were all alike—feeling totally ridiculous there with our packs and gear, snowshoes and cross-country skis among all the skiers. Thus, in true mountaineering fashion we ascended Brundage Mountain by plunking ourselves down in the chairlift and watching the scenery go by as we went up.

Yet, at the top our "raison d'etre" became radically different from that of the skier—this mountain would be our home tonight. The vista of snow-smothered trees and crystal peaks struck us anew with the sense of nature's vast majestic indifference.

Mist during the early morning had transformed the first inch of snow into a light layer of crystals that swished into the air at the whisk of a ski pole. A delightful sound! And as we all stood there swooshing and whisking, Odd decided it was time to lead the party onward. So, with a fleeting glance at the chairlift, we slid off to look for a place to build snow caves. Mid-mountain is usually best, Odd had told us, because it is likely to be the warmest. But Brundage is peculiar, being equally warm on top, so we would set up near the top (especially since skiers don't appreciate a snow cave in mid-run). We dropped slightly down the far side of the mountain for privacy.

There we split into four groups, and I landed in the largest—a group of six. That meant a lot of people to help build the cave, but it also necessitated a large cave. We went to work. Since it was brilliantly sunny, most of us were soon digging in our shirt sleeves and the process began to bring out the child in all of us. Surely in a time of dire need, digging a snow cave would be no party, but on this sunny day, it was a great game. The trouble was, all six of us couldn't fit in that tiny hollow, so I was delegated the task of kicking the chunks of snow headlong over the mountainside toward McCall. Onlookers soon discovered that my kick had a nasty left hook.

Once we had finished, plastic tarps were spread over the floor. Only one problem: on dragging in all our sleeping bags we discovered our cave wasn't quite big enough. So out came the bags, pads and tarps, and the disgruntled cave-carvers went at it again.

By this time the sun had moved enough to leave our cave in shadow, and the absence of that warm glow made a surprising difference. Cold and anxious to be through with the work, we were grateful for Odd's warning that we would need extra warm dry clothes for "after the digging." After the tarps were spread for the second time, we donned our spare clothes quickly and headed up hill to meet the rest of the group.

A few yards up, we discovered the sun again, still brilliant. Hunks of cheese and salami, nuts, candy and dried fruit appeared out of the packs and were quickly devoured. Odd complimented us on our caves and let us in on the fact that those snow-smothered trees all around us were not really trees at all, but Norwegian trolls hiding from the sun so that they wouldn't explode or turn into rocks. Tough life, being a troll...

It was 2:30. At 3:30 the local air service wanted to make a practice emergency air drop, so until then, we were free to ski, rest, eat, whatever.

I wanted to know more about the trolls, so Odd explained that they had originally come to Idaho via the Greenland Ice Cap, across the Northwest Territories, and down the McKenzie River. He had originally won their trust by speaking Norwegian to them and finding a lost baby troll one winter. In gratitude, they had offered him a lovely troll princess for one night, but Odd declined the offer when he discovered that she had a cow's tail.

Suddenly a plane was circling overhead. Odd and another man in our party quickly set off smoke flares to demonstrate how to signal a position. Orange billows spread across snow and sky, making it clear why this color had been chosen as the standard emergency signal. The plane hovered above us once more, and then, suddenly, down came a pack. It landed less than five yards from us. To any group of *real* survivors this would be like a gift from heaven.

Odd was already rummaging through the pack. Out came the caribou parka and reindeer pants (in case any one of us should change our minds about Odd's offer) as well as extra sweaters, parkas, a sleeping bag, and that infamous "anti-exposure suit." Bruce winced...

Odd quickly explained that Bruce would be in no real danger, and advised him to don the suit. As we buried him, he was to cover his face with his arms to allow breathing space, and when we had piled on enough snow, he was to try to dig himself out.

"Now, what was the name of your closest relative?" laughed Odd as the shovels went to work. Bruce was lying on his back and soon disappeared beneath a mound of snow. "Can you breathe, Bruce?" Odd would yell. And always the answer came back fainter and fainter, but affirmative and re-

assuring. He had been buried with a ski pole sticking up, so that he could signal with it in case he panicked.

Finally, Odd gave the great mound a couple whacks with his shovel. "Now try to dig yourself out!" he called.

After about a minute, a little snow flew from the top of the mound. Then everything was still

"Are you all right, Bruce?"

A tiny voice came out of the snow. "I can't breathe...My chest..."

They had him out of the drift in seconds. "God, was that scary!" he gasped, blinking the snow out of his eyes. "The snow didn't feel heavy 'til I tried to move, and then...Boy, that last minute I really freaked out!"

"You can do it if you don't panic," Odd assured us. "If he could have shoved the snow away a little at a time, slowly, *without packing it*, he could have gotten out.

Bruce was lovingly guided up to our communal fire, where he kindly shared the impressions of his own private avalanche. Already it was growing cold and dark. Odd spoke of many wonderful human encounters he had had over the years...the importance of companionship. "Ve are none of us here to be heroes," he was saying. "Ve are not male and female—ve are all human beings, here to help each other, to learn from each other. If there is anything I have that you vant, I vill give it to you, because I am not stingy...because I have received many many things from people I never seen before..."

We huddled closer to the fire, nibbling our high-energy foods and wondering just how warm those little ice-boxes were really going to be.

Eventually the time came to find out. But back at our snow cave we decided to boil some water first and have a little cocoa before bed. The snow in the cooking pot was slow in melting. A half hour went by and there was little water—and only barely warm at that, something Odd had warned us about when he discussed melting snow for water. Already some of our cave-mates had given up and crawled into the cave. To our surprise, they called out that it was much warmer in there. Candles in little niches in the walls were giving off heat, and the yellow glow from the opening looked more inviting than the black around us. We drank our tepid cocoa and scrambled in.

Actually, sleeping in a snow cave proved to be a pleasant surprise. With insulation from the pads and plastic under us, we were perfectly warm. Of course, we did have down bags and slept in our long johns, but when its -10° outside, comfort in a snow cave is nothing to sneeze at.

So, with our packs piled high against the opening, we slept soundly until the first shafts of light began to beam through. We had survived! But then, the prospect of crawling out of that pocket of warmth was none too pleasant. However, talk about hot coffee at the bottom of the chairlift sparked our incentive and we were soon up and dressed. We ate breakfast, packed, and were soon skiing on our way.

"Nature ... nature is beautiful. But Mother Nature does not care about you! She in indifferent."

Half the group decided to ski down the backside of Brundage into McCall rather than accept the humility of taking the chairlift down the mountain. I had an appointment to meet, though, and my skis were too thin to dare the crusty descent of Brundage, so I accepted the chairlift as a rather unglamorous way to end my exploit on the mountain. On reaching the bottom, however, I felt better. Odd had come down the same way half an hour before—already off to another lecture!

And so ended our introduction to winter survival with Odd Bjerke. Admittedly, it was tame—a very controlled kind of winter camping experience—and not really "survival" at all. And yet, should any of us ever be snowbound and without equipment in the wilderness, we can always say: "Well, I camped in this stuff once before, so I guess I can do it again."

FIRST TIME OUT

BY BOB EDWARDS

Bob Edwards is an electronic engineer, working with computers, in San Jose, Calif. and an active member of the Sierra Club's local ski touring section. His two young sons first got him interested in winter backpacking and camping. Now all three of them are hooked on the activity. Here Bob describes their first winter camping experience.

"But Dad," pleaded Juan, "Why can't we go backpacking in the winter time?" Could this be Juan, aged nine, my youngest son, who just that spring had had to be urged up the trail in no uncertain terms? Now, in late September, he and Tejas, aged 11, had cornered me.

"Yes, Dad," said Tejas, "You don't expect us to sit around here in the city every weekend breathing smog, do you?"

"All winter long?" added Juan.

"True," I hedged, "but we don't have proper equipment. We only have tube tents, light dacron sleeping bags and summer clothes. And besides, nobody goes into the Sierra in the winter, the snow is too deep."

"What about skiers?" asked Juan, skeptically.

"Well," I answered, "Skis cost a lot of money, ski resorts are crowded and expensive, and we can't afford it."

That closed the subject for the time being, but a seed had been planted in my mind.

The following April, I received an unexpectedly large income tax refund and decided the best use I could make of the money would be to spend it on good backpacking equipment. A good tent and down sleeping bags were what we needed. Then that little seed in my mind started to take root. Down sleeping bags are pretty expensive, but a bag suitable for winter didn't cost that much more than a summer bag. The same held true for a tent. So we bought the heavier sleeping bags and tent.

All summer long we luxuriated in being warm at night while others were chilly, and our tent seemed like the Hilton after those miserable tube tents. We had heard about cross-country skiing, and as fall approached, we were anxious to learn more about it.

We have been members of the Sierra Club for years (that's where we learned how to backpack), and were pleased to learn that the Sierra Club had a ski touring secton. Looking through the schedule, we noted that they had courses in ski touring, winter survival and snow camping. The three of us were eager students at every class. We listened to all of the experts' opinions about skis, waxes and other equipment, then went to the sports store and were pleasantly surprised at how inexpensive ski touring skis were in comparison to downhill skis.

A day in November finally came when we were saturated with theoretical knowledge and simply had to try out our new skis. I will pass mercifully over that day except to note that in some ways skiing was easier than we had thought, and in other ways a whole lot harder. A couple of weekends later we took some instruction in cross-country skiing, and decided that maybe it was a viable means of transportation after all.

We realized that what we wanted was a winter substitute for summer backpacking. Two skills would be required: the ability to ski cross country (which corresponded to hiking in summer) and the ability to camp overnight in the snow, far from civilization, using only what you've carried on your back. After many day trips on skis, we felt reasonably sure of the first part, but what about the second part? Could we actually camp on top of that deep snow? Could we build a fire? How would we stand the bitter cold? What if it snowed? By now we knew enough to realize that you don't get away with many mistakes in winter. Sure, in summer you can make every mistake in the book, and probably the worst that can happen is that you'll spend a miserable night. But not in winter. When that sun goes down and that chill wind comes up, everything had better be right or else! Could I subject my boys, now 10 and 12, to such danger? Those were the thoughts that weighed on my mind.

Fortunately, the Sierra Club had scheduled a beginners' snow-camping weekend, and we were signed up for it. Before you could go on the snow-camping weekend, you had to attend an evening's instruction first. This consisted of good, solid practical advice on what to bring (and what not to bring), how to detect hypothermia and what to do about it, and more—much more. It was a long session, but crammed with information. The gist of what we learned was: you could not only survive, but you could be comfortable and have a good time if you had the proper knowledge and equipment. Well, our equipment was good, and, as far as the knowledge was concerned, we were learning.

The night before leaving, we went over all our equipment one last time. Of course, we had the things we normally took for summer backpacking: the sleeping bags, insulating pads, Primus stove, cooking utensils, food, tent, maps, compass, etc. But what I especially wanted to check were the new winter things: the down jackets with hoods, the extra wool stockings, the wool mittens with waterproof overmittens, the thermal underwear, the wool shirts, wool hats and the snow goggles. (Good Lord, don't forget the wax for the skis!) The packs felt somewhat heavier than in summer.

Since the purpose of this trip was snow camping, the skiing was kept to a minimum—about three miles, much of it across the frozen and snow-covered surfaces of Lower and Upper Echo Lakes near Lake Tahoe. We were at the trail head at the appointed hour. Most of the 12 other members of the party were already there. Our leader, Bill Firth, gave us a final equipment check. The spare ski tip (in case of a broken ski)? Yes. The wax scraper? Yes. First aid kit? Yes. Flashlight? Yes. Everything was in order, so off we went.

It was a good day for ski touring, moderately cold and overcast. We had learned from experience that a clear sunny day, while beautiful, makes the touring more difficult. You have to wear goggles to avoid snow blindness; it's harder to wax your skis properly so they won't slip in sunny spots and stick to the snow in the shady spots. But worst of all, on a sunny day you tend to get too hot and sweaty when you're skiing. Then when you stop to rest, suddenly you're cold and clammy. No, we preferred a cloudy day.

It was about noon when we arrived at our campsite above the shore of Upper Echo Lake. We selected a spot that was in moderate forest and near a stream, so we could get water without having to melt snow. We had purposely sought out a place where the snow was deep because some of us wanted to try our hand at digging snow caves. Although the boys and I had brought our tent, we wanted to see if we couldn't dig a snow cave and use that for our night's shelter. We had heard that snow caves are a warm and elegant shelter. Some of the party talked of building igloos, but that seemed a little tricky for me.

Right after lunch we started digging. I had a small collapsible aluminum snow shovel which worked just fine. Soon I had a shoulder-deep hole about three by four feet in dimension. Then I started tunnelling horizontally. The first two or three feet were easy, but then I had to lie down in the tunnel to dig further. As I dug, the boys helped by throwing the snow up out of the hole. We took turns at tunnelling and throwing the snow out. After a couple of hours, we had a cave big enough for two people, but I was getting very tired. It's no easy task to lie on your side and try to dig and then push the snow out of the tunnel past your body. So I climbed out of the tunnel to stand up and stretch my cramped muscles. Outside, there was a rather chilly wind blowing which made me realize I was soaking wet. And, of course, the boys were wet, too. You get wet partly from the perspiration generated by your hard work, and partly from lying in the snow while you dig.

I knew enough about the hazards of hypothermia to realize we were asking for trouble if we didn't do something quickly. Now seemed like a good time to brew up some hot bouillon soup. So I got out the Primus stove and sent Tejas to the stream for water. The wind was getting stronger and I was starting to shiver, so I set up the stove down in the hole which was the entrance to our snow cave. There it would be out of the wind. Tejas came back with the water and I made him and Juan sit in the cave out of the wind. Bill Firth stuck his head over the edge and said,

"How are you doing?"

"Pretty good." I replied, "But we're going to take a little break and have some hot soup. Do you want some?"

"Sure," said Bill, "I'll be back in a couple of minutes."

I primed the stove and lit a match. I was shivering pretty hard and it was not easy to strike the match, but it lit and the stove flared up. The heat felt good. When the priming flame began to burn low, I turned on the valve. At this point the stove is supposed to fire up. Nothing happened. The priming flame flickered out. As anyone who uses such stoves knows, this happens now and then. The solution is simple: take the cleaning tool, poke the fine wire into the little hole in the nozzle to clean it, pour more fuel into the priming cup and re-light. I knew that. But somehow it seemed like an insuperable problem now. I was shivering too hard to ever use that cleaning tool. The boys were shivering, too, I could see. Had to do something. My mind worked so slowly. Pick up the gasoline bottle...open it...pour some on the stove...give the bottle to Tejas to close...open the match jar...take out a match...try to strike it...match breaks...get another...(I'm never going to make it)...strike it. The match lit and the stove flared again.

"Now this time, stove," I muttered, "Work, damn you! I turned the valve and the little stove roared into life. That has to be one of life's more comforting sounds. I knew we were going to be all right. I put the pan of water on the stove and we all huddled around it, teeth chattering. Soon our soup was steaming hot and we all drank it greedily. We had almost stopped shivering when Bill came back.

"Are your clothes wet?" he asked.

"Yes, they seem to be," we answered.

"And you're shivering, too. Aren't you?"

"Well, yes. A little," we replied.

"It was wise of you to stop and make some hot soup," Bill said, "because you're on the verge of hypothermia."

"Now finish your soup," he added, "And then go over to my tent and put on dry clothing."

As I was changing into my dry clothes I realized that if we went back to our cave, these clothes would soon be soaking wet again. Then we'd be in real trouble because this was our only set of dry clothes. At this point I realized that discretion was the better part of valor and decided to put up our tent and forget about snow caves for the time being.

By now it was 4:30 and the other snow cave diggers had come to the same decision I had, and were also erecting their tents. That nice dry warm tent was a welcome sight indeed. I had wondered if those thin little wire tent pegs would work in the snow, and figured on using the skis and ski poles for tent pegs if they didn't hold. Turned out they held just fine.

Cooking in the snow can be a little tricky. We tried setting the stove on an inverted pan and then surrounding it with an insulating pad to keep the wind from blowing all the heat away. This was working well until we noticed the whole thing leaning crazily like the Tower of Pisa. The pan was getting warm and melting the snow. So, we transferred stove and dinner to the blade of the snow shovel. This was broad and flat and did the job well until the shovel got warm. Then slowly the shovel, the stove and our dinner began to slide majestically down the almost imperceptable slope. Well, no wayward shovel is going to escape with the dinner while my two hungry boys are standing by, so it was quickly retrieved. At last, we were able to sit down to a well-earned supper of turkey soup followed by shrimp creole. For dessert, we had large cups of hot chocolate.

About that time, Bill Firth came by and checked our tent and sleeping arrangements. He declared that everything looked fine and that we should have a comfortable night. Darkness comes early in winter and by 6:30 it was almost dark. Nobody even suggested building a campfire, and I could see why. The snow was covering all the dead wood on the ground that one normally uses in the summer time. Besides, all of us felt tired and those warm sleeping bags almost seemed to be calling us. People drifted off to their tents, and one hardy soul off to his snow cave. By 8:00 everyone was in bed. Our little backpackers' candle hanging in the tent cast a friendly glow as I pulled off my boots and pants and slid into my down bag. We lay and talked awhile by the light of the candle while the wind outside began blowing harder. What an incredibly good feeling to be lying there warm and comfortable with the wind howling outside! I fell asleep.

I awoke much later. The candle had gone out, the boys were snoring, and I could hear light rain falling on the tent. Rain! That would certainly make miserable skiing tomorrow. But I was cold, that was what had awakened me. Why was I cold in a down bag that was supposed to keep me warm? Then I noticed that I had rolled off the insulating pad. I moved back on the pad. Much warmer. But I was still chilly. Cold air around my neck and shoulders. Now's the time to try the hood on my mummy bag (I had never used the hood before). I put it over my head and pulled the laces so that only my nose was sticking out. Now I was warm again. But I was just the slightest bit frightened. It is a strange feeling to know that not only your comfort, but your very survival lay within the narrow confines of that mummy bag perched on top of a tiny insulating pad. I went back to sleep.

When I woke again, it was light, my watch said 8:15 and I could still hear light rain falling on the tent. But it certainly seemed cold for rain—I could see my breath. Finally, my curiosity got the better of me and I sat up and peeked out. Rain indeed! There were 18 inches of new snow and it was snowing heavily. What had sounded like the drizzle of light rain was really the large snowflakes hitting the taut surface of the tent. I lay back down and warmed up again. Sitting up had let cold air down my back. Soon the boys woke up and lay there laughing and talking about the 18 inches of snow that had fallen on us during the night. Nobody wanted to get up. It was so nice and warm inside the bag, and so cold out there (eight degrees below zero, to be exact).

Let's see now, all I have to do is unzip the bag, leap out, pull on my pants, take the down jacket out of its stuff bag (I had been using it for a pillow), put on the jacket and I'd be OK. It's like jumping into a cold lake. The only way to do it is to go ahead and do it—quickly. OK? Now! I leaped out bravely and pulled on the pants. I think they were frozen solid, but I got them on. Now the jacket. My Lord, it's like ice! Zip it up, put up the hood. I began to warm up. Now put on your boots. They really were frozen, even the laces were stiff. But no dallying now because Mother Nature is making it quite clear you have an urgent appointment outside. By the time I had come back, I was really quite warm again. The boys were more reluctant to brave the rigors of the cold, but soon they were up, too.

The first order of business was to fix breakfast. Where was the stove? Right where we left it last night—only now it was under 18 inches of snow! Could this lump be it? No, that's the gasoline bottle. How about this one? That's a pan, we'll need that. And so it went. After some poking and digging we rounded up all our things. The water bottle was frozen solid and we could not get the ice out. We got the stove going (no trouble this time), and soon had a breakfast of hot oatmeal and hot chocolate. My backpacking experience had taught me to keep breakfast simple. We like to get packed up and going, and hate to clean up after an elaborate breakfast.

Our tent had survived 18 inches of snow beautifully. Shaped like an indian tepee, it was too steep to allow the snow to pile up on it. Some of the other, more conventionally shaped tents were sagging badly. The Brave One, who had slept the night in his snow cave, swore he was warm and dry, and hadn't even been aware of the night's storm.

In looking back at this, our first snow camping trip, we have to laugh at some of our mistakes, and thank our lucky stars that other mistakes didn't kill us. Naturally, we're now careful not to leave things lying around the camp where they can get buried by an overnight snow. But one thing we particularly never allow ourselves to do is get wet, or even slightly overtired. That one brush with hypothermia was enough for me.

We have gone on to many other ski touring and snow camping experi-

ences since then. The boys and I have come to feel as much at home in the High Sierra in the winter time as we do in the summer. We've camped in blizzards as well as fair weather, intense cold as well as mild temperatures. We haven't dug any more caves, and still haven't tried to build an igloo. But we did spend one very pleasant night in the shelter at the base of a large spreading fir tree. Although we've gained experience, we never go out alone. We always go with at least two other people. If I'm ever tempted to go alone, I recall how nearly impossible it was to light that match when I was merely on the verge of hypothermia. Then, I was in no real danger because help was near-by. But alone—no, thank you.

This summer, the first thing we noticed about summer backpacking was how easy it was compared to snow camping. So much less equipment to worry about, lots of daylight, no cold. But we noticed other things, too, like dusty trails, mosquitoes, pesky bears that raid food supplies, swarms of other backpackers. In fact, as we were standing beside the trail to let a long, dusty mule train pass by, Tejas said, "You know, Dad, I think I like winter camping better."

"Yes," chimed in Juan, "Why can't we go snow camping in the summer time?"

Where was the stove? Under the 18 inches of snow that had fallen overnight.

3 THE ART OF WINTER CAMPING

"A PECULIAR CRAFT"

BY MILES BECKER

Twenty-eight-year-old Miles Becker is the outdoor program director at the Athenian School, a private boarding school in Danville,California, near Oakland. Formerly with Outward Bound in California, Washington, Oregon and Massachusetts, Miles has extensive experience as an outdoorsman.

Winter camping is a peculiar craft. It is not essentially complex nor difficult, and when pursued with prudence and understanding no sensible person will encounter difficulites that cannot be avoided or overcome. But winter is the most unforgiving season, and the traveller in the wilderness in winter who acts carelessly or in ignorance will find that the consequences of those acts are swift, often unpleasant, and sometimes brutal.

To illustrate, imagine two parties leaving a mountain resort in March for a weekend tour. The experienced party leaves early Saturday morning. They know that the weather is expected to deteriorate, but they are up for an adventure, and are equipped and prepared to enjoy it. They have been touring for many years.

The less experienced party hasn't heard the weather report, and although none of them have been touring or winter camping even a year, they have a great deal of sophisticated and expensive equipment and a great deal of confidence. They don't get an early start, and since it's obvious to them that the party ahead is "on the route" to Mount Wherever, they ski in the other party's tracks. They also don't pay much attention to the map.

The first party, meanwhile, is making excellent time, but not on the route to Wherever. They left that route after a few miles, heading off into some "interesting looking country" one of them had seen from a distance the year before.

By late afternoon it has begun to snow. The first party is setting up camp in a broad valley, many miles from where they started, but only a few miles from a road. The less-experienced second party has just realized that the tracks they were following don't lead to Wherever, and furthermore, can hardly be seen. They have made poor time, stopping often to rest, and haven't come far. Nevertheless, no one can clearly remember how many streams or ridges were crossed, or which direction Mount Wherever is in, since no one has seen it for almost an hour. But after long argument one of the party convinces himself and the others that he knows just where they are, and points out that in order to complete the tour they have to make it at least to a certain lake that day. The others agree that they should "get on with it", and the lunch that was postponed because of the late start is postponed again. They ski on.

While the second party hurries into the gloom, the first party is in its tent (and half of them in their sleeping bags), involved in a discussion about whether leek or onion soup goes better with freeze-dried lasagna. The cook settles the issue with the observation that anyone who gives him any more trouble can damn well cook the dinner himself, and finding an old package of oxtail soup in his pack, cooks that.

An hour and a half later it is getting dark and still snowing The second party has given up on the lake. Only then do they realize that they are missing someone, and that no one knows how far back he is. Setting up camp is slow business, in the dark, with numb hands. Even down jackets, when damp with sweat, are cold.

Half an hour passes. The missing person arrives (with the tent poles). They finally get the tent up, and three of them crawl in, very tired and very cold. The fourth goes for water. The three in the tent argue about whether they should bother to cook or just eat the lunch they didn't eat during the day. They decide to cook, but discover that the stove is nearly empty, and someone forgot the gas. In the meantime the fellow who went for water is a little clumsy from hypothermia and falls in. By the time he gets back to the tent he is shivering violently. Someone remembers something about hypothermia and blood sugar, and they give him candy. He doesn't eat much.

While all of this is going on, the first party is drinking some after-dinner cocoa. Two of the party members are energetically discussing the relative merits of pin bindings and Silvretta cable bindings for high late spring tours, while another reads and the fourth prepares to demonstrate that popcorn after freeze-dried lasagna isn't such a bizarre idea at all.

Another half hour passes. Someone in the second group, concerned by the incoherence of the fellow who'd fallen in the water, but not thinking very clearly himself, finally remembers that a victim of hypothermia cannot produce heat. He zips his bag together with his friend's and gets in with him. He tries to get the friend to eat more candy, which the friend does, a little, but the others are too tired to eat. By and by, dehydration, exhaustion and hypothermia overcome discomfort, and they sleep.

About the same time the first group finishes its second batch of cocoa (a luxury) and the popcorn, which they all admit wasn't such a bad idea after all. Before too long they, too, are asleep.

The following morning it's still snowing and the experienced party decides that plodding about in two feet of new powder with a visibility of 50 yards isn't that appealing. They ski down the valley to the road, and a few hours later are in a favorite bar telling lies and making plans for the next time.

Getting water from a stream in winter can be a complicated procedure. Obviously, extra care must be taken not to fall in.

And the second group? There are many possible endings to their story. It's likely they died–some of them at least. But perhaps not. Perhaps they were lucky and got away with no more than a very frightening and miserable experience. But the lesson is the same regardless: that ignorance, overconfidence (arrogance) and carelessness are terribly dangerous in winter, but that winter is not inherently dangerous at all.

The mistakes the second group made may seem small, like not eating lunch in order to "save time", or assuming that the party ahead is going where you are, or neglecting to check the weather report, or skiing with too many clothes on, or pushing on late in the day or in bad conditions simply to complete a tour. In the summer this kind of error would probably not matter much. In winter, though, a few small mistakes can bring disaster. But once again, there is no need to make them.

The recent boom in wilderness travel, combined with the philosophy that equipment makes the man, has brought a large number of people into the woods who are very well equipped and very ill prepared. Caution and good sense can't be bought in a ski shop, nor can care and skill. And no amount of nylon and down will take their place. The novice should go slowly and carefully, and be sure never to exceed the limits of his experience and ability. The freedom to go where you will in the wilderness in winter brings rewards that are well worth that patient effort.

COVERING THE BASICS

BY MIKE HARDING

Mike Harding is general manager of Mountain Traders, a backpacking/ climbing/ski shop in Berkeley, Calif. Mike started his wilderness experience in 1959 on the slopes of Mt. Fuji while in a typhoon. He's been an enthusiastic rock climber, year-round mountaineer and ski-tourer ever since.

Among the uninitiated, winter camping has the image of being a rigorous, complicated activity. It doesn't have to be, of course, as long as one knows the practical, common-sense techniques and procedures of winter camping. Here I will cover some of the basics, using a question and answer format for simplicity's sake.

● **What clothes shall I wear?**

Here in the Sierra region of California, where I go skiing and winter camping, layers of clothing are preferable to a single heavy garment. I am partial to wool fishnet underwear, turtleneck shirts, wool bicycling jerseys, tightly woven knickers, wool Pinnochio socks and sweaters. When a wind breaker is necessary, I don my floppy waterproof cagoule which hangs well below my knees. I've also adopted a pair of wind pants (not waterproof) for wear when windy or when very warm. When warm, I wear my long-johns with the wind pants knickered. Down clothing is very warm and light but in a 32° rain storm beneath a cagoule, it gets soaked. Tall gaiters that extend to the lowest boot hook or eyelet keep my lower leg warm and boots free of snow. A wool balaclava and Dachstein mittens with waterproofed nylon over-mitts complete my effective if campy costume. Around camp I wear down-filled booties with overboots.

A word on boots. I prefer to ski with three-pin bindings. This necessitates a three-pin boot. I've found that in the Sierra my feet don't get cold as long as I'm moving and am wearing dry socks. There are several styles of touring boots with double snow tongues and above-the-ankle uppers that appear warmer than the traditional track shoe.

● **What do I do if I get cold?**

"Put on your hat!" As much as 1/3 of your body's heat loss is from the head, so obey this old maternal injunction.

Often tourers find they get cold during a lunch or "brew-up" time. One remedy is to put on a dry shirt or change socks as damp clothes are chilly.

Staying warm is a lot easier than getting warm. Soon after camp is

One way to keep warm on a winter camping trip — exercise.

chosen and shelter secured it is wise to change socks and boots. A pair of down-filled slippers within a pair of overboots is wonderfully warm and a great morale booster. If you're still chilled, vigorous exercise for a moment or two, then jumping into a fluffed-up sleeping bag is wise.

Naturally, a quickly boiled cup of soup or sweetened tea or hot jello often works wonders. A shot of alcohol isn't recommended even though you may feel instantly warm for a moment after you've had it. Alcohol dilates the capillaries, thus increasing blood near the skin surface and extremities for a quick cooling. With the sudden warmth comes perspiration. When the blood slows down, you can often be clammier and colder than before.

• **Where's the latrine?**

Sanitary facilities or "area" should be located conveniently close to camp, yet well sheltered for maximum comfort. The area should be selected with some thought to prevent water pollution in spring and summer. Since the ski tourer melts snow for water he need not set his camp site near lakes and streams. Some groups have suggested that toilet paper be burned after use or, better yet, not even used. The suggested alternative is snow. Sounds rugged but it's natural and clean.

• **Where will I camp tonight?**

Unlike the summer knapsacker whose choice is dictated by the location of water and competition from YMCA, Boy Scout and Wilderness club groups, the winter camper is free to camp almost wherever he wants. Since snow to be melted for water can be collected without leaving the shelter, the winter camper's considerations are shelter from wind and storm and keeping away from obvious avalanche paths. The cave digger will seek the deep drifts in which to burrow. The tent pitcher will stamp out a site in a corner shielded by big trees or boulders. The view lots on the ridges and points are less desirable. Sites in the trees are to be avoided when branches are heavily laden with snow, as are camps on the snow bridges above streams or on the ice of a lake.

• **How do I get a fire built?**

Building fires in the snow is a real bother when you can use a stove instead. It should also be understood that fire scars wood, uses up rapidly diminishing high altitude soil cover, and is dirty.

If you must cook or gain warmth from an open fire, start by gathering sap from the lodgepole pine. In the Sierra that's not much of a problem as it grows at nearly every elevation ski tourers will travel.

A handful or two of sap is advantageous. Try to locate dead twigs that break easily; if too wet they will bend and burn slowly, if at all. After collecting a sizeable twig pile, gather pencil-size and thumb-size wood. Stamp an area down four feet or so in diameter, protected from the wind, and free from snow falling from boughs above. Cover a small area (1' x 1') with the least burnable wood. Get your smallest and driest twigs together in teepee fashion and place the sap cautiously so that it will burn quickly and run on top of the wood. As the fire grows, add larger pieces until the fire is the size you need.

A tripod of three sticks with a piece of clothes hanger wire to hold the pot works better than placing the pot directly atop the fire. After the fire is dead, scatter its remnants carefully so that others can have the benefit of a virgin wilderness experience, too.

• **What do I do if I get cold in my sleeping bag?**

There are four basic points to the sleeping scene: (1) Waterproof ground sheet beneath. (2) Adequate insulation beneath you: ½" Ensolite, type M, (3) A fully fluffed and dry sleeping bag with no light holes, (4) A canopy directly above you but not on you: for example, a tent or snow cave.

If you have all four and have done them in good style and are still cold consider: (a) isometric exercise in your bag; (b) eating some super sweet food and exercising; (c) putting some clothing on or over you at the cold spots inside the sleeping bag; (d) snuggling closer to your buddy (with, perhaps, a word of intent before you do so). Frequently, when touring with several companions, we place the "cold sleeper" between two "hot bloods."

● **The nights are so long in the winter. What do you suggest I do if I can't sleep?**

Knit.

A candle lantern provides warmth, illumination, and a degree of cheeriness. Make sure there is adequate ventilation or you'll sleep forever. During bleak days and long nights in a tent or snow cave, cooking, food, and staying warm become major preoccupations. Writing, reading, card games, sketching, poetry reading, and conversing have perked up many otherwise drowsy days.

● **What's cooking?**

The difficulties of housekeeping in a 5x 8 tent filled with two wool sweater-clad humans, two sleeping bags, two packs, etc., make *cordon bleu* cookery impractical. Meals that require two pots, like spaghetti or meat and potatoes, are difficult to serve when both pots are hot. Single pot meals like stew or shrimp pilaf minimize fuel consumption and cooking time. A thick soup is always welcome for its liquid saltiness and ease of preparation.

For some years now I've used an Edelweiss cook set. This unit consists of a white gasoline stove, windscreen, and two double boiler-like pots with a large lid that can substitute for a frying pan. A thin sheet of plywood or asbestos placed beneath the stove is handy to prevent the whole unit from disappearing down a snow hole.

A simple meal would begin with soup in the small pot; the entree would be stacked atop the soup pot and indirectly warmed. When the soup is ready, the entree pot would be switched atop the stove. As soon as the soup pot was empty it would be filled with water for making tea. After the entree is consumed the pot would be scoured out with snow and then filled with water (for washing, drinking, and beginning the morning meal).

If snow must be melted, a large pot is suggested as well as a snow bag. The snow bag is filled to the brim and dragged into the tent or cave. As snow is needed for water it's taken out of the bag and placed in the water pot to melt. To prevent scorching of the pot, a bit of water should be in the pot when starting to melt snow. If no water is available, add snow gradually to the hot pot until the snow melts and forms a good pool. [For more information about cooking, see "Food and Cooking", page 57.]

SKIS, SNOWSHOES OR BOTH

BY LESLIE HURLEY

The mode of travel is of great importance to the winter camper. Few people are more qualified to discuss the subject than Leslie Hurley. He is co-author, with William Osgood, of *The Snowshoe Book* and *Ski Touring*. In addition, he has had considerable experience in Ski Patrol work, off-trail rescue and winter camping as a participant, an instructor in the US Army and now as a physical education instructor at Norwich University in Northfield, Vermont.

What are the best skis to use on winter camping trips? As the *Nordic World* booklet *Nordic Skiing Gear* points out, it certainly depends upon who is using them, under what conditions and how much of a load is being carried on the back. Many winter-tripping articles seem to assume that the reader has a choice of every type of ski, pack, snow condition and weather, and all he or she has to do is set up the slide rule conditions, apply a formula, record the results, then pick up the gear and take off to a honeymoon with Nature's virgin winter wonderland. Tain't so though. Most ski tourers inclined to try overnights will use the skis they have. Then it becomes a matter of common sense to match the trip with the equipment. Choices of terrain, snow conditions, route, temperature ranges to be expected and one's own physical abilities and those of his companions—skill-wise and stamina-wise—must be considered.

If you have never camped in snow before and live in snow country similar in temperature and snow depth to the area where you hope to camp, then camp first in your own backyard. Never mind the meals, just set up and practice camping out. Put your skis on, ski around your own boundaries, circle back to your selected site and make camp. In the morning, pack up, shoulder your gear and ski back around your plot, then dismount at the back door, kick the snow off your boots, take off your pack, open the door, put the pack down on the kitchen floor and start to analyze the operation. Did your skis "warble" as you skied with that heavy load? Did your poles seem too short because they went deeper into the snow? Did you break them by putting too much weight on them as you tried to get up with that heavy load? Did your skis sink too deep in the snow? Did you poop out making that little circle? Were you so damn cold during the night that you didn't sleep a wink and are now very sleepy in the nice warm kitchen?

Many lessons are remembered longer from doing things *wrong*. It is so easy to recall the wrong moves and experiences and much harder to consciously stop and remember what we did right. The correct moves slip by unnoticed.

SKIS OR SHOWSHOES

My own personal considerations when debating what to take (skis, snowshoes, or both) on an overnight winter camp-out are:

1. If I am going to be in deep snow (knee to hip deep) when I step off my skis then I always take along a pair of Bearpaw snowshoes. If I were going to travel over a mile and stay longer than one night I would carry a pair of the aluminum frame shoes to save weight.

2. If the trip will be only a day long, out and back, and in steep New England type mountains (heavily forested) I would use my mountain skis with partial edges and, of course, a Silvretta type binding. I am not at all hesitant to use jumping toe irons with cable to reduce weight just because I am used to them and feel confident with them. I exercise judgement in route selection to fit the equipment. On this type of trip I would then be prepared for bridging narrow gullies and miniature ravines and I could be a little bolder in my bushwhacking with sturdy equipment. I would most likely be packing climbing skins, just in case.

3. If I were on a gentlemen's tour—no real rough bushwhacking or abrupt terrain changes—I would use my no-wax skis and to heck with wax. Planning on two or more nights out, I still carry snowshoes—at least one pair for every two people in the group. This arrangement works nicely. There is no need to worry about different footgear for snowshoes. They can be worn with whatever you are wearing for skiing—especially as they are not going to be used for long periods of time. This trip with my "no waxers," by the way, presumes there are no time, speed, or certain-number-of-miles-to-cover requirements. I would *not* use Trak Bushwhackers (a specially-designed, wide, short—150 cm—no-wax ski) for this trip because I do not feel stable on such short skis when carrying a heavy pack.

4. I would borrow my friend's Trak Bushwhackers for short ski orienteering trips over rough terrain in preference to showshoes if I were concerned with time. I would be apt to use them also when exploring in spring snow conditions in tricky terrain. They can be fun under the right conditions but I feel their uses are limited.

5. I would not take snowshoes along on a ski overnight if the snow was only deep enough so that when I prepared the bivouac site I could easily pack it down with a few sidestepping passes over the area. I wouldn't take snowshoes along if the snow didn't come much above my ankles when I stepped off my skis. Extreme depth of snow isn't always critical. Spring snow conditions or snow packed on windward slopes often is compacted enough so you can walk on it without skis or snowshoes. In these cases, snowshoes would be dead weight.

6. Whether or not I was going to camp out, I would go conventional with tough touring skis with a variety of waxes, a scraper, thermometer, cross-country boots (low or high but with snow cuffs) on any trip on which I anticipated changing snow conditions, open and wooded terrain, long runs, gentle climbs and switchbacks, and lots of stops to enjoy the views (actually for me those stops are excuses to catch my breath). I would use pin-type pole-operated bindings and any other energy-saving device that did not add weight. I would only debate about poles: weight and strength versus lightweight and efficiency. On the fun trips I would certainly use the lighter pole. You do have to know what you can do with your poles in the way of extracurricular activities—such as using them for a seat, as tent poles, as a climbing or belaying aid, fighting off wolves or spearing fish. Some poles might be universal in their uses but most are not. I would change to a wider basket ring only when I knew I would be pushing down hard on the poles when climbing in deep snow.

7. I would use snowshoes exclusively on winter overnights involving narrow trails, thick woods, steep climbs, sharp curves, rough descents, deep snow and heavy loads. I would, however, carry metal ski poles as they are stronger. As to the style of snowshoe, my choice would probably be the tailless variety (a modified Bearpaw) if much bushwhacking is involved. I would use Ojibwas or Alaskan Trails if sticking to the trails. In breakable crust conditions I would stay home, or venture forth and pray a lot. I would definitely carry ice creeper attachments for trouble spots.

IN SUMMARY

My experience, while not so diversified as to include high alpine expeditions, is enough to make me feel confident that these ideas I have stated are valid, although they may not be popular with the purist ski tourer. I once felt that I could do anything and everything on skis, but age mellows one, as does hard work when combined with concerns for safety with others of unequal abilities. I found snowshoes compatible with skis and skiers. Gosh, I don't even mind them in the same column, especially if the snowshoers volunteer to break trail.

Also, in our mountain rescue work both in practice and for real we have found snowshoes extremely useful. For one thing it is much quicker and easier to get a stable platform on snowshoes when need arises such as for a belay on an evacuation litter.

OVERNIGHT SHELTERS

BY JIM RENNIE

Jim Rennie is the outdoor program coordinator at the University of
Idaho in Moscow, Idaho and a regular contributor to *Nordic World* magazine.

Of key importance to the winter camper is the type of shelter to be used
for the night. There are several types of shelters possible, with the most
popular choice being a tent. Keeping dry and warm is essential to enjoying an
overnight tour, and a tent should serve this purpose.

After many long winter nights in tents, I have come to some conclusions
regarding the advantages of each kind. Weight is always a factor in any item
of gear carried, but large tents have my vote for winter use. There are a
couple of reasons why. Foremost is comfort. Winter nights are long, and 14
hours may be spent in the tent at one stretch. With no room to shift in an
economy-sized tent, life can become very tedious. There also is the alarming
tendency in a two-person tent to wake up in the morning with the tent wall
pressed up against your face as the newly fallen snow has caused the tent to
sag. Three- or four-person tents, particularly the pyramid design, are great for
stretching room. Many an evening has been spent with six or eight people in
a party all piling in one four-person tent to talk or play cards. It's a nice alternative to bed when the sun goes down at six o'clock.

In pitching a tent in the snow, you will soon discover that the stakes that
come with the tent are too short for winter use. This can be resolved by
placing the pegs in sideways and stomping snow on top of them. Ski poles and
ice axes also are good for staking out tents. It will be handy to dig a hole in
front of the tent entrance. This hole will enable the tent inhabitants to sit
down in the tent entrance while taking boots off outside. It's easier to take
your boots off in this manner, and it keeps the snow outside of the tent.

With the availability of more time, many winter campers try their hand
at snow shelters. It eliminates the chore of carrying a tent, although you may
have to carry a shovel in its place. Simple snow shelters can be made in an
hour or two. There are many natural features of the landscape that can be
utilized for this purpose. Trees and rock cliffs can form a part of the shelter.
The enterprising camper then builds additional walls to make an enclosure.
Often a hole can be dug about two feet deep first and walls built from the
top of the hole. The roof can be supported by skis laid across the walls and
a tarp spread over the skis. To top off this shelter—literally—snow is spread
on the roof over the tarp to add insulation. It's a simple shelter to build and
ideal for one-night sojourns.

Longer tours may demand something more permanent, particularly if you are fond of the base camp approach where you camp in the same place each night and merely take off on day tours. You don't have to be an engineer to build a fairly elaborate snow shelter. It takes time and patience, but the reward is more than worth the effort.

The principle behind igloos and snow caves is quite simple. The snow serves as insulation from the air. While snow is cold, it is seldom colder than about 30 degrees. Air, on the other hand, may drop to 30 below. A person in a snow cave or igloo, therefore, only needs to be prepared to sleep in temperatures generally in the 20's.

Igloos are the traditional form of snow shelter that most people are familiar with, and the most familiar type of igloo is the usual round shape.

This type, however, is more difficult to build than a square or oblong type. Igloos, like the snow shelters described earlier, can be greatly facilitated by digging a hole first. Digging out a hole means less cutting will have to be done on the blocks of snow for the walls.

Spring igloos are generally much easier to construct than ones in mid-winter due to the natural compaction of the snow. Loose powdery snow may have to be thoroughly packed before it can be cut into blocks. The foot thick blocks can be cut with a shovel, a snow saw (designed for this purpose), or a ski tail. Be aware, however, that ski tails can be broken in this manner! The blocks are then arranged pyramid fashion to form walls. Holes are plugged with loose snow. The trick is to gradually place each block a little farther inward as the wall is built, so that the top may be cemented with one or two large snow blocks. The most efficient entrance would be a small tunnel underneath the wall, but removing a few of the lower snow blocks will suffice also.

It will take about a day of work to complete an igloo unless you have lots of friends to help. The floor should be levelled to provide maximum comfort, as it will become extremely hard after a night's use. Candles will provide enough lighting to make the interior friendly, and small holders can be cut out of the walls. A small stove used to cook dinner will warm the interior remarkably, but some sort of ventilation should be maintained whenever using stoves.

Once night falls and you're warmly tucked into your bag, with the stove giving off a friendly roar, you begin to appreciate the igloo. It won't blow down, it's as spacious as your demands require, and really a friendly place. Before blowing the candles out, stick your head outside for an exterior look at the igloo. The light shining through the snow will make the igloo look like a large glowing mushroom in the night!

The ultimate in shelters is the snow cave. Caves tend to be warmer, larger, and simpler in construction than the igloo. You do admittedly become soaking wet while building the cave, but once it is built you will begin to appreciate its advantages.

Lots of snow is a basic requirement for good cave construction. Preferably, the site should be on a relatively steep hill. This not only assures a thicker roof, but it makes removing snow much easier, as it can be dumped over the edge of the hill and out of the way. A typical four-person snow cave will require from four to eight hours to construct. Shoveling snow can be rather tedious work, so it is recommended that you have large snow shovels. Grain scoops also work well. The small backpacker snow shovels often seen in outdoor catalogs are handy for tight corners and smoothing ceilings, but the larger shovels reduce the work of moving vast quantities of snow.

In principle, the cave is supposed to trap the warmer air in the cave and prevent circulation of colder air from the outside. To achieve this, the cave living area must be higher than the cave entrance. Generally I dig six feet in horizontally, then six feet up. From this standing position a shelf waist high is levelled out on which the campers sleep. With plenty of snow, there is no limit to the size which the cave can be made. If the day is not right for touring due to bad weather, minor improvements can be added daily and the cave gradually enlarged.

The first thing you notice in a cave is the absolute quiet. Sound will not penetrate the snow and a storm can be raging outside while the candles nary so much as flicker inside. Small shelves can be dug out of the walls to hold the candles and to store personal items. A tarp on the floor is essential to keep bags dry.

No doubt the first cave you build will have problems. Here are some of the classics:

Rain is falling on your head. This is caused by small pockets in the ceiling collecting water. If the ceiling is smoothed over this shouldn't happen. Also watch the cave temperature. Cooking will raise the temperature and cause more melting. One cave I experienced had 10 people in it and even without cooking the temperature never went below 39 degrees.

The roof is sinking. This is caused by the roof being too thin to stand the warming and cooling of the cave interior. The ceiling will sink lower and lower each night until it chases you out or the cave is enlarged. Ceiling to roof thickness should be a minimum of two feet.

The entrance becomes snowed over. This is hard to prevent if it is snowing hard, but excess snow should be shovelled out before bed. The middle of the night is no time to arise and have to dig a new entrance. Ventilation in the ceiling is also important, particularly when cooking. A small hole bored to the outside will help as long as it is kept clear of snow.

The cave collapses. This is very rare and not as serious as it might sound. A cave that is too near the surface does not have much strength in the ceiling which may break or melt away. Caves should be dug deep to prevent this. A dome shaped ceiling will also increase strength.

Snow caves as well as any show shelter will greatly facilitate exploring the back country. It is amazing how friendly the snow can become. It is a means of travel, a means of shelter, and you can even melt it and drink it. Every winter camper should try a snow cave or igloo at least once.

STAYING FOUND

BY CARL SMITH

It's one of the more important skills for anyone who's going to travel in the winter woods. Carl Smith is a physicist-mountain climber from San Carlos, Calif., who has plenty of experience with map and compass in the wilderness. He participated in the Sierra snowshoe crossing that is described in "Sierra Crossing" (page 111). For further evidence of Dr. Smith's ability with a compass, read that article.

Staying "found" is a fairly simple matter if one has some familiarity with topographic maps, and if one is observant of the terrain. Of course, travel through heavily wooded areas or white-outs does present some special challenges.

For most back-country areas, 15 minute ("quads") or 7½ minute ("octals") topographic maps are available. These are your "guides" in finding your way in the back country. Topographic maps of the United States are produced and sold by the US Geological Survey. For areas west of the Mississippi River order from US Geological Survey, Federal Center, Denver, Colorado 80225; for areas east of the Mississippi, from US Geological Survey, Washington, DC 20242. Topographic maps of Canada may be purchased from the Map Distribution Office, Department of Mines and Technical Surveys, Ottawa, Ontario.

In order for these maps to be useful, one needs to develop a good working familiarity with them. The USGS has a brochure which describes the symbols used on the maps, but the real nitty-gritty is a working familiarity with contour lines. What does a deep notch in a ridge look like on a map? How steep is the area? What is the elevation gain between two points? Why do trails often parallel contour lines or zig-zag back and forth across them?

Study a topographical map of an area you are familiar with and see what the peaks, stream courses, and lakes look like on the map. With some experience you'll be able to look at a map and readily envision the terrain. Bunched up contour lines close to a stream will tell you something about travelling through that area. Finally, there's a certain amount of enjoyment and delight in pouring over topographical maps, but be careful, for you can easily become a map freak.

In getting ready for a trip, study a topographical map of the area in which you'll be travelling. What is the elevation gain from the roadhead to your proposed camp? What is the general direction from the roadhead? Where will the sun, if visible, be along most of the route? What topographic features (ridges, valleys, peaks, etc.) will you cross or be close to? What will they look like with a snow cover?

DON'T START OUT LOST

After packing, organizing, and probably a number of hours of driving, you'll reach the roadhead. In the hurly-burly of last minute things, take the time to look at the map. Don't start out lost, in other words. Orient the map with your compass so north on the map coincides approximately with compass north, and locate the roadhead. Look around to see if you can spot topo features such as a close ridge or stream course that are shown on the map. What about that peak you thought from map study you should be able to see along most of your route?—can you see it now?

As you leave the roadhead, take a couple of looks back at its setting. Are you going to have any trouble finding it when you return? (I've seen roadheads where you had to be 10 feet from the cars before they were visible.) It's worthwhile to fold your map to a convenient size with the travel area showing. A plastic bag over the map will keep snow off and protect it from extensive handling. Tuck it inside a shirt or somewhere close at hand.

While you're travelling and taking in the scenery, note the topo features you see, such as an open area, or a ridge. Then, when you take a few minutes' stop, take out the map, quickly orientate it with the compass, and try to spot your location. Identify the topo features you've observed since you last looked at the map. This constant looking and map peering may sound like a lot of work. Not so, for it quickly becomes second nature and one notices topo features almost automatically as one is enjoying the scenery.

The above procedure works well in open or semi-open terrain, but how does one do it in a wooded area? Even if one is following a blazed or marked trail (metal tags on trees), one should pay attention to direction. Is this the direction the map shows? Following the tracks of a previous party is easy but perhaps they were headed elsewhere. Finally, there is the case where you're in a wooded area without a trail or track, and few topo features (such as a stream course) to follow.

PROPER COMPASS PROCEDURE

With the map and compass figure out the direction you wish to travel. Orient yourself with the map. Unless otherwise noted topographical maps are printed with north at the top of the sheet. So all you have to do is to hold the map and compass together and rotate the map until the top is due north.

Each map also indicates the degree of magnetic deviation (about $16°$ in California) and the direction, east or west, in which this deviation occurs. For accuracy, this deviation must be taken into account. It means the needle of the compass is not pointing to true north but to magnetic north. To account for this, rotate the map the indicated number of degrees west if the deviation is east and east if the deviation is west. This may sound complicated, but remember, the compass is off—not the map.

Now set the rotating part of the compass housing so that the arrow points in the travel direction while the compass needle coincides with the

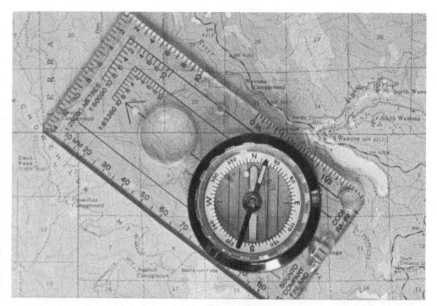

Navigating with map and compass. Note compass needle pointing to the magnetic north and compass housing set off to the northwest in the desired direction of travel. (OMPhoto)

marked north. Sight a tree 100 feet away in your travel direction and walk to it. Take out the compass again and sight the next tree. Don't get so engrossed with this compass procedure that you miss seeing an attractive icicle or perhaps a snowflower in a melted spot.

Two comments apply to this travel technique. Travel via compass is relatively slow; one keeps feeling that one really should be there by now. Also, it's easy to get your direction off by as much as 40° if you're not careful. So check the compass often. Even with careful attention to direction it's difficult to travel to a precise spot.

Though usually not recommended, it is sometimes expedient to travel in white-out conditions. A white-out may be fog or a snowfall that is heavy enough to limit visibility to 100 feet or so. Lay out your route on the map and get a compass bearing. Here is where your previous study of the map pays off. Note the topo feature you expect. If there are any treacherous areas (steep gullies, etc.) maybe you should hole up and wait for the weather to clear. Carry the compass in your hand and check your directions every few minutes. One feels very sheepish in coming across one's own tracks and realizing that one has made a loop.

As the visibility varies, note clumps of trees, rock masses or other features that you may then spot on the map and check your location. A bit of caution: watch your physical condition and that of your party, put on more clothes if you're at all chilly, and proceed with certain deliberation. Should you or someone in the party get tired, stop and camp!

IF YOU BECOME LOST

Lost? Congratulations, it's pretty difficult to do if you've been paying attention to the map and the terrain. But if it happens, stop, sit down, have a bite to eat, sip some water, view the scenery, and relax for a couple of moments. Pull out the map and orient it with your compass. Recall what you've seen since your last look at the map—a stream crossing or a meadow perhaps. Or maybe you've been in fairly flat forest: the map will show green vegetation with few contour lines. Lay out your travel direction since you last fixed your position. With all these bits of information you should be able to make a fair estimate of your present position. Consider that you may have misidentified something. Discuss your position with your companions. Usually as one sits, eats, relaxes and looks over the map, one's location becomes clear.

Let me conclude with some advice on compasses and topographical maps respectively:

• **Compasses**—The old army lensatic compass is excellent, but quite difficult to find now. The cheap imitation of this fine compass has very poor damping—i.e., one has to wait five minutes for the needle to stop swinging. The Swedish and Finnish compasses consisting of a rectangular plastic plate attached to a circular needle housing are good, especially the ones with liquid needle-damping. The fancier versions of these and also the Brunton compass used by geologists are bulky, expensive, and not necessary. With any compass, remember to hold it away from metal objects.

• **Maps**—Although topographic maps are about the best for back-country travel, they are sometimes out of date on roads. If you're going to travel in a National Forest, obtain their map if only for roadhead information. Regarding map accuracy, remember that although a lot of careful work goes into a topographical map, the terrain has been drawn from aerial photographs. Thus, modest scale gullies in wooded areas and features smaller than the interval of the contour lines may not show up.

FOOD AND COOKING

BY VIRGINIA MEISSNER

Mrs. Virginia Meissner of Bend, Oregon has the credentials and experience to write about almost any subject pertaining to ski touring or winter camping. For the past 25 years she has logged hundreds of miles per winter on cross-country skis as a snow surveyor (measuring the snowpack) in Oregon's storm-bound Cascades. One of a handful of women in the US doing snow survey work, she started out by helping her husband Jack take snow measurements on McKenzie Pass in 1949. She's been measuring this and other snow courses ever since. In addition, she lectures on ski touring and winter camping at Central Oregon Community College, and has her own cross-country ski school. Her husband Jack is now a ski instructor. Her son Ernie, 20, is a junior national champion cross-country skier and was on the US biathlon team last winter.

Essentials for survival in a winter camping situation are shelter, warmth and water. Next to these comes food, which provides energy and warmth for the body and incentive for the mind. The thought of an appealing, hot dinner at the end of a day of ski touring provides psychological encouragement to keep moving along the trail.

In picking a campsite it is important to choose a place which is protected from weather dangers such as wind and avalanche, which has available wood if a campfire is to be used (with a gas stove this will not be essential), and which has water. Water is obtained much easier from an open stream or hole in a lake than it is by melting snow. However, when you're winter camping you may indeed have to melt snow for your source of water.

SOURCES OF WATER

Since water is essential to the winter camper (you can go longer without food than water), let us consider first the various means by which you can get water on a camping trip:

1. **Water from an open stream.**

Running water from a fast running mountain stream is the most appealing source, and it may present no problem at all in the spring when melting snow lets you walk right to the edge of a stream. But earlier in the season you may find a delightful stream which is 10 or 15 feet down with straight up-and-down snow banks on either side. The obvious danger here is that the snow bank will collapse and you will get an unwelcome dunking in ice water.

To obtain water in this situation I like to carry a can which has a length of nylon cord tied to it. The cord is then strung through the basket of your ski pole and used "fishing pole" style to obtain water.

2. Water from a frozen lake.

In mountains such as the Oregon and Washington Cascades water can usually be reached within about three feet or so by digging a hole (with a ski pole, ski, stick or hands) straight down through the snow on the lake. Under the top layers of snow will be layers of slush and eventually water which will rise in the hole so it can be dipped out.

3. Water dripping from rocks (during the spring).

When the sun is warm enough to melt the snow, water can often be found dripping from the lower edges of rocks. Set a can under the drips and enjoy the sun while the can fills.

4. Water at the edge of a melting snow bank (again, during the spring).

In much the same manner as water dripping from the rocks, water can be easily collected in thawing weather by finding places where it is running from the edges of melting snow banks and hunks of ice. With either of these last two methods be sure to gather enough water in the afternoon to last for the next morning because if there is freezing temperature overnight all running water may be frozen solid until the sun warms it again late the next morning.

5. Melting snow.

Wet snow is easily melted in a pan over a fire. Start with a small amount and keep adding more snow until you have as much water as you need.

Cold powder snow presents more of a problem. The saying "don't burn the water" is very true here because the water content of light, cold snow may be very slight. When melting this kind of snow for water, start with just a small amount. Keep stirring as you go and add a little at a time until you get water started in the bottom of the pan. Then keep adding and stirring as you go. As water builds up in the pan the process becomes easier.

It takes a lot of cold powder snow to make a cup of water. "Don't burn the water" actually means don't let the pan burn while you're trying to melt enough snow to get a layer of water covering the bottom.

Purification of water is not the problem to the winter camper that it is becoming to the summer hiker. If there is any reason to believe that the water you get is not pure enough to drink, it can be purified by boiling, using halizone tablets, iodine or chlorine.

COOKING FIRES

Choice of cooking fires is a matter of personal preference and what fits the situation? The trend now is towards carrying a little gas stove. But I think it is important to at least know how to build a wood fire in the snow in case you get injured or become lost. In both cases, a fire would be necessary for survival. Emergency situations aside, a wood cooking fire will provide warmth which may be welcome on many occasions.

Of course, depending on the area you're in, there may be several reasons (such as the ones listed below) why it may not be possible to build a campfire or cooking fire. In these situations the gas stove is a necessity.

● In some areas of heavy use in national parks and national forests the use of wood for fires is restricted. This can be checked out with the ranger in the local area where you are going.

- The snow camper, after a period of heavy rains in an area, may find everything is so drenched and wet that it is very, very difficult to find anything that will burn.
- Stormy, windy weather conditions may be such that you will want to cook inside of a tent. Be sure you have adequate ventilation.
- In case of a campsite above timberline there may be no trees, therefore, no wood.

If a wood fire is to be used and the snow is deep, the first thing a novice will discover is that after an hour, or sooner, as the fire burns, the snow under and around it melts and the fire begins to sink. After a while the fire will be way down in a hole. To prevent this, foot pack the snow as hard as possible at the site of the fire. Then lay a base of logs, bark or other wet stuff that will not readily burn. Build the fire on top of that. The thickness of the base will depend upon the length of time you expect to use the fire.

A cooking fire does *not* have to be a big fire. All that is needed is a fire big enough to heat the underside of the pan. It is also much easier to handle pans and to work near a smaller fire.

The procedure for starting a fire in winter is almost the same as that used in summer. Start with dry tinder, which can be:

- Dry twigs ("squaw wood") from the underside of trees.
- Pitch from trees.
- Inner dry wood.
- A candle.
- Commercial fire starters (fire stick, fire ribbon, etc.).
- Homemade fire starters (egg carton, sawdust, paraffin with a wick).
- Ski wax.

After the tinder is started (keep adding enough until it is well lighted), add kindling. Kindling consists of slightly larger pieces of wood. Increase the size of wood only when you are sure it will burn. After all of this is burning well, larger fuel can be added. A winter fire needs "tending." Keep it pushed together and keep enough small wood and embers around the larger wood to keep it going.

Coals are much better to cook over than flames. Pans and food do not get as black, and coals offer a more even temperature.

There are many, many kinds of compact gas stoves on the market for you to choose from. Manufacturers and store personnel will be able to tell you about the different kinds. Certainly, it is desirable to have at least one gas stove of some kind in a party of campers in case a wood fire cannot be started.

COOKING UTENSILS AND APPROACHES

What are you going to cook in? Manufacturers have provided us with a wide range of cooking kits. These usually include a couple of sizes of kettles with a lid, a frying pan, and sometimes a cup. Choose whatever fits your needs and the amount of weight which you can carry. The needs of one person will necessarily have to be lighter than those of a group of people where weight can be divided among the group.

I like to carry two or three sizes of pans (these can be large pans, with bales, which will nest together). Be sure you have a lid or foil to cover the pans. A teflon-coated frying pan is a good choice (for a trip of several days, not just for overnight).

Another very useful item is a plastic shaker. Once you have carried a one-quart plastic shaker you will wonder how you ever got along without it. It can be used for mixing lemonade or powdered milk, or for shaking instant pudding, and you will find many more uses for it as you go along. It is also handy for packing envelopes of drink mixes, etc. in the pack.

Each person should have his own cup and spoon. Beyond that, plates, forks, etc. are a matter of personal choice. A tablespoon is nice to have when cooking. If you plan to cook pancakes or eggs, be sure to take something to turn them with.

There are at least four different ways of cooking food:

1. The most basic way is in a pan or kettle. "One-pot" soups, stews, or dinner mixes are excellent choices on winter camping trips. I'll remind you again to be sure to take a *lid* for your pot. At any high altitude the food will "never" get cooked without one, especially with everyone sitting around eagerly waiting to eat! Food and water will boil much faster at any time if you use a lid and the liquid will not boil away as fast, either.

2. Cooking on a stick presents an opportunity to let the imagination take over. There is no end to the combinations of things which can be toasted, baked or broiled on a stick. Anyone who thinks a stick is just for a wiener or marshmallow has a lot to learn! The first step in cooking on a stick is to learn that a good cooking stick has *two* ends—a pointed, tapered end to poke things on and a larger (1" or more) blunt end for wrapping things around. Bread sticks made of a biscuit mix, wrapped around a stick, baked over coals and filled with butter or jam are excellent with any meal. Competition gets fierce to see who can get the best golden brown one without burning it. Stick cooking gives everyone a chance to do their own cooking.

3. Foil cooking in the coals is something which takes more time—time to get good coals, and time to bake the foil-wrapped food after it is put in the coals. The results are well worth it. Foil cooking is best done when you know there will be lots of time and when people aren't so anxious to eat that they can't wait. Foil packets can be made up at home so that they are all ready to use.

4. Reflector cooking is another type which requires time and patience. This can be done with a commercial type reflector oven (which may be too heavy and bulky to carry), with a foil type reflector (devised wtih sticks and foil) or against a flat rock or log. Try reflector cooking in the summertime first, then progress to winter camping with it.

WHAT FOODS?

Now to get down to the matter of what foods. Be sure to take plenty. People will usually be hungry after exercise and in cold weather, calories are required to provide body heat and energy.

Some factors to consider in the choice of foods are:

● How much time will there be to cook?

- What kind of weather is likely? (In cold, stormy weather something hot will be wanted as quickly as possible. In warmer weather you can take more time.)
- Will the people who will be preparing the food be tired?
- How much does the food item weigh and how much weight can the group (or individual) carry? (Glass jars and cans are much too heavy.)
- What utensils are required for preparation?
- Can the food be eaten just as it is?
- Can it be eaten by just adding cold water?
- Can it be eaten by just adding boiling water?
- Can it be cooked in one pot or on a stick?
- Is the mix complete in one package?
- Does it require that other ingredients be added?
- Does it require more than one pan?
- Does it cook quickly?
- Is there a minimum of waste and garbage to carry out?

Everyone has their own likes and dislikes in food and this should influence the choice of food, especially when you are in a cold winter situation when it is essential that everyone eat adequately.

When planning what food to take, think in terms of breakfast and dinner as meals to be cooked, and lunch as something to probably be eaten somewhere along the trail. One good way to plan lunches is to give each person a "snack-pack" to be carried in a handy place so that he or she can nibble along the way. It is better to eat several times along the way. This not only gives an energy boost, but it gives a chance for a rest which some people will need. Others will welcome the break as a chance to observe scenery, take pictures or study maps.

Good foods for a "snack-pack" are things such as "gorp," freeze-dried fruits, dehydrated fruits, raisins, jerky, pepperoni, smoke sticks, cheese, salami, chocolate bars or bits, nuts, sunflower seeds, hard candy, fruit drops, fig newtons, "hard tack," raisin fruit biscuits, wheat thins, ginger snaps, sesame seed bars, cheese 'n' crackers and peanut butter (in squeeze tube).

PLANNING MENUS

Breakfast and dinner menus can be made up to personal preference. It is good to have either a hot drink or instant cup-of-soup to drink while the rest of the dinner is cooking. This relieves a lot of "when do we eat?" comments.

The basic staples to put into your pack are: salt, pepper, sugar, cinnamon, margarine, (onion flakes are really handy, too) candle or fire starter. Each person should carry waterproof matches and a jack-knife or sheath knife.

Most foods you will need can be found at the local supermarket. The next time you go to the store make a point to look as you go up and down the aisles to see just how many suitable foods there are on the shelves. Sporting goods stores and specialty shops carry a great variety of freeze-dried and dehydrated foods especially packed for the backpacker and camper.

Here is a suggested list of foods to get you started. You will find more and more as you get more interested in winter camping and discover your food likes and dislikes.

DRINKS

Bouillon—beef, chicken, onion, vegetable.
Instant orange breakfast drink.
Instant lemonade, and other fruit flavors, with sugar already added.
Tea bags and instant tea.
Instant hot chocolate—the kind with milk already added.
Instant or freeze-dried coffee.
Powdered milk.
Powdered chocolate milk.
Fruit-flavored gelatin.

BREAKFAST

Granola.
Instant oatmeal—several flavors (mix with powdered milk at home).
Instant hot cereal of any kind.
Quick cooking oatmeal (cook with raisins soaked overnight).
Biscuit mix.
Pancake mix.
Instant applesauce.
Dehydrated applesauce (cook the night before).
Freeze-dried fruits.
Bacon.
Brown 'n' serve sausage (will keep in cold weather).
Hominy grits and corn meal mush (make the night before, fry for
      breakfast).
Powdered eggs.
Rice.
Jam—in squeeze tube.
Syrup.

LUNCH

"Snack-pack"—see list already given. These things may also be incor-
      porated into other meals.

DINNER

Instant cup-of-soup—many flavors.
Dehydrated soups—many flavors and brands.
Packaged dinners (check to see if they are complete in one package):
      Skillet dinners
      Noodle dinners
      Spaghetti dinners
      Rice dinners
      Macaroni dinners.
Instant mashed potatoes.
Hash brown potatoes.

Instant gravy and sauce mixes.

Ham—pre-cooked.

Bac-o-bits.

Dried chip beef.

Corned beef

Jerky or salami (cut up and add to mixes).

Meat (some will keep in cold weather).

Instant puddings.

Dumplings—made of biscuit mix and added to soup or stew.

Large variety of freeze-dried dinners (such as beef stroganoff, etc.).

Dehydrated vegetables and salads (some have to soak a long while).

After the menus are all made out and the food bought, comes the packaging project. Plastic sacks were the best thing ever invented! Pack and re-pack. Many things come in their own foil or plastic container. If not, open the box and re-package in a sturdy plastic bag. Be sure to cut out and include the directions for preparation. Take a felt marker and write on the outside of the plastic sack what is in it. Next, take the menu and put all things required for a single meal in a large plastic sack and mark with the day and meal (e.g., "Friday dinner"). This way all of the food packages do not have to be opened every time, only the one which is a complete package for the meal at hand.

Then make up individual "snack-packs" for each person for each day. These could be put all in one bag. But if the trip is more than one day long, you're better off to separate the packs as then the people in the group will be less likely to eat everything at the beginning of the trip and run out at the end. After all food is packed, make up and stick in some out of the way place in your pack an emergency food packet to be used only if you should have to stay out longer than expected. This can include bouillon, tea bags, chocolate, nuts, etc.

Don't take more food than you need, but be sure that you have enough. After a few times out you will develop many little hints of your own, ways to have better meals, ways to cut down on the amount you carry, and what you like and don't like.

LOOKING AFTER THE ENVIRONMENT

A few points in closing on looking after the environment when you're out winter camping:

1. As a matter of sanitation, select toilet facilities away from streams, lakes and camping areas.

2. Burn toilet paper or put in garbage to carry out.

3. Burn all waste paper, etc.

4. Carry out foil and cans and anything else which won't burn.

5. Wash dishes away from source of water supply, and use non-polluting soap.

6. Do not bathe or wash hands directly in the water supply.

7. Leave a neat, clean campsite for the next person. The mess covered up with snow will be there for next summer's hiker when the snow melts.

RECIPES

Baking mixes: You can get several brands at the supermarket or make your own. Uses:

Biscuits
Bread Sticks
Pancakes
Bannock (fry-pan bread).
Dumplings
Thinkening for stew or gravy
Fruit cobbler.

WHEAT-SOY BAKING MIX

1½ c. whole wheat flour
2 c. white flour
½ c. soy flour
½ c. wheat germ

6 tsp. baking powder
1½ tsp. salt
2/3 c. powdered milk
¼ c. brewers yeast

Mix all together. Mix with water when ready to use. Makes about six cups.

BAKING MIX

2 c. whole wheat flour
1 c. rye flour
1 c. cornmeal
½ c. soy flour
1/3 c. sugar

4 tsp. baking powder
2 tsp. salt
1½ tsp. soda
2/3 c. powdered milk

Mix all together. Mix with water when ready to use.

BANNOCK

1 c. flour
1 tsp. baking powder

¼ tsp. salt
(increase ingredients as desired)

In camp: Stir in enough water to make firm dough. Shape into flat cakes. Lay in warm frying pan. Hold over heat until bottom forms crust. When firm, turn over and finish cooking.

CHOCOLATE MILK

8 oz. powdered cocoa
1 lb. sugar

12 oz. powdered milk

Mix all ingredients. Makes enough to go with eight quarts of water. Divide into eight parts. Each package then requires one quart of water.

FRIED CORNMEAL MUSH

1½ c. boiling water
½ c. cornmeal
½ c. water

½ tsp. salt
½ tsp. sugar

Mix dry ingredients and cold water and add gradually to boiling water, stirring constantly. Cook until thick, stirring. Cover, cook over low heat 10 to 15 minutes. Pour in small pan. Chill overnight. Slice and fry. Serve with butter and syrup.

SYRUP

1 c. brown sugar   ½ c. water

Boil sugar and water three to five minutes. Add four tablespoons butter.

CREAMED CHIP BEEF

Make cream sauce from mix (or from butter, milk and flour). Add chip beef and serve over toast, biscuits, or instant mashed potatoes.

CREAM SAUCE

2 Tb. butter   1½ c. reconstituted milk
2 Tb. flour

Melt butter, stir in flour. Add small amount of milk and stir until smooth. Add rest of milk little by little, always stirring until smooth before adding more. Cook a few minutes, stirring constantly.

RUSSIAN TEA

1¾ c. instant orange breakfast drink   1 pkg. instant lemonade mix
1¾ c. sugar   1 tsp. cloves
1½ c. instant tea   1 tsp. cinnamon

Mix all ingredients. Use two teaspoons per glass, less for a cup. Pour in hot water.

"GORP"

M & M's   Dried fruits
Peanuts or other nuts   Raisins

DUMPLINGS

2 c. biscuit mix   2/3 c. milk (or water)

Mix into soft dough. Drop by spoonfuls onto boiling stew or soup. Cook uncovered over low heat for 10 minutes. Then cover and cook 10 minutes longer. Makes 10-12 dumplings.

STEW
(mixes for dumplings)

Start with any kind of soup and gravy or sauce mix. Add onion flakes, parsley flakes, or whatever you like. Add noodles if desired. Cook and, when boiling, add dumplings and cook.

BREAD STICKS N' SAUSAGE WRAP

Heat brown 'n' serve sausage on stick. Wrap biscuit dough around hot sausage on stick. Bake over coals, turning as the dough browns.

JERKY

1½ or 2 lb. lean boneless beef
(partially frozen to slice thinly)
½ c. soy sauce
1 Tb. Worcestershire sauce

¼ tsp. pepper
¼ tsp. onion powder
1 tsp. hickory smoke flavored salt

Trim all fat from meat. Slice across grain—¼" to ½" thick. Combine all spices and sauces in bowl and mix until seasonings are dissolved. Add meat strips and mix to coat all surfaces. Let stand overnight in refrigerator. Arrange meat on racks in oven (not overlapping) or on cake racks set in shallow baking pans. Dry meat for four to seven hours at lowest oven temperature (150° to 200°) until it has turned brown, feels dry and is hard.

Pat off any beads of oil. Store in airtight bags or jar. Store at room temperature.

GRANOLA

4 c. quick cooking rolled oats
3 c. whole wheat flour
1 c. white flour
1 c. wheat germ
1 c. rolled wheat

1 c. chopped nuts
1 tsp. salt
1 c. vegetable oil
1 c. honey or brown sugar
½ c. water

Optional: sunflower seeds, sesame seeds or raisins.

Mix dry ingredients. Add oil, honey and water; mix well. Mixture should be crumbly and more water can be added to make bigger crumbs. Place in two large flat pans and bake in a slow oven (250°-300°) turning every 20 minutes to keep mixture from becoming too brown around the edges. Bake about 1½ hours or until crisp and golden brown. Cool and store in airtight container.

RICE DESSERT

Add raisins or other stewed dried fruit to soft cooked rice. Eat with milk, sugar or cinnamon.

THE ENVIRONMENT

BY DAVE BECK

Among other things, Dave Beck is an avalanche consultant, ski tourer, winter camper, lover of the winter outdoors and author. The following article and the one on page 103 are adapted from his book *Ski Tours in California,* published by Wilderness Press.

The word *wilderness* used to mean an unknown, lawless area. Today it usually means an area devoid of busy highways and other works of modern man, which may or may not be an official wilderness area where government has forbidden motor vehicles and other benefits of technology. Wilderness is a place where we can find a quiet, peaceful moment outside our usual surroundings.

A ski-tourer and/or winter camper should understand why he should and how he can minimize his impact on the landscape. If he cares about the land he skis and camps on, and hopes to continue to ski and camp on it, he must know what effect his actions have.

Most ski tours take place in fragile ecosystems, where the ecological balance is easily upset because the growing season is short and vegetation is relatively sparse. Both conditions exist in the mountains of my state, California. (Most ski tours in the state are in the mountains.) Since California has very little summer rain, the moisture available for plants at higher elevations comes from melted snow. The growing season doesn't start until the ground is wet from meltwater, and it ends when moisture becomes scarce, usually by midsummer. Above 4000' to 8000', depending on where you are in the state, the kinds and amount of vegetation begin to decline. To preserve the mountain touring environment, skiers must make a conscientious effort to have as little impact as possible.

LITTER

The most obvious form of impact is litter. Small objects dropped onto the snow quickly become buried, only to pop to the surface later when the snow melts. Nothing is more unsightly in the spring than an area where a careless touring party has lunched or camped. Keep bags in your pack and parka pockets for litter, and use them. Carry out *everything* you take in. Furthermore, we are all responsible, to some extent, for one another's actions. Just cleaning up after yourself is not enough. If you come across others' litter, carry it out. If you encounter others littering, gently correct them.

PRIVATE PROPERTY

If you stay in a cabin or a hut—whether by reservation or because of emergency—leave it in better condition than you found it.

CAMPSITES

In choosing a campsite, pick one summer campers are not likely to choose. Fortuntaely, the best winter campsites are typically well away from the streamsides and lakeshores which summer campers prefer. In spring, when the snow is low, the tourer usually looks for a grassy spot to pitch his tent. He shouldn't, because he will probably damage the soil and the vegetation. Damp ground is easily compacted, and vegetation that is just starting to grow is very vulnerable. Damp ground makes a cold camp anyway. Camp on a bare, *sandy* spot or on snow. Don't camp in wind-drainage channels, where the cold air flows down at night. Even a large meadow can become a "lake" of cold, damp air.

SANITATION

Sanitation is a major problem. On snow-covered ground you can't dig a latrine. Use a spot at least 50 yards from streams, lakes and summer-use areas. Burn your toilet paper (some skiers use an eyedropper of stove fuel to ignite it). Otherwise the paper will last a long time.

WOOD AND FIRE

Weathered dead trees (snags) make a valuable contribution to the mountain scenery; they should be left alone. Some scenic snags are hundreds of years old.

Even in heavily used summer areas below timberline, snags should be left alone.

Don't harm live trees by cutting them or driving nails into them. The era of the bough bed, moreover, has passed. Modern snow campers carry an Ensolite or foam pad.

If you build a fire on bare ground, do so in a flat, sandy area. Never build a campfire against large rocks. Fire-blackened boulders are particularly unsightly; the fire scars can last for years.

It is best to build a campfire on a low platform of rocks, which must be strewn about, blackened sides down, when you leave. Then no one can see where your fire was.

The mountains in winter have a quieter grandeur. If a skier wants to get to know them, he must first respect them and learn to live with them. Campers who act loudly or thoughtlessly will miss much, from a glimpse of a pine marten to the sound of the wind. Travel softly and leave as little trace of your passing as you can. Not only will future campers benefit from your behaviour, but you will come closer to the spirit that probably drew you into the wilderness in the first place.

PUBLIC ACTION

There are other ways you can help preserve the touring environment. Proper management policy for public lands is very complex. Issues are clouded by personal and financial desires, by lack of information and by disagreement over what the public really needs. Investigate land management and planning in the areas you camp in; express your opinions to the governmental managing agencies. Quite often a project is well underway before the public shows any interest. Controvery could often have been averted and money saved if everyone who cared about an area had spoken up earlier. Learn about public hearings and attend them—or at least find out what occurred at them. You should particularly find out what the costs and benefits of a proposed development are expected to be, what the environmental-impact statement says, and what alternative plans exist. Express yourself. Whether there will be a good environment for future ski-tourers and winter campers depends on us.

4

EQUIPMENT

TAKE WHAT YOU NEED

BY HUGH BOWEN

"The fewer things I have to carry, the better. I like to ski! All the rest of that stuff is a means to an end for me. I wouldn't carry any of those things if we were really space age moontripping. I'd ski all day and then I'd reach in my back pocket and my food would come out and my tent would pitch itself and my bag would loft automatically. I wouldn't carry anything if I could get away with it."

—James Jakovec, North Face, Palo Alto, Calif.

Since you can't "moontrip" in winter, choosing the proper equipment becomes critical. Unfortunately, the array of survival gear that is "necessary" can bewilder beginners who are already scared by the dangers inherent in winter camping. But equipment need not deter you. Rental prices are reasonable (they're listed later in this article) and equipment experts from some of the top mountaineering shops in Northern California tell you, in the following pages, what gear is needed for your first ski-touring, winter-camping overnight.

The amount of equipment you can comfortably carry on your back depends primarily on your skiing ability, but also on how well your skis fit you and the terrain. Hold the weight under 30 pounds for your first trips, if you can.

"Ideally, someone who is thoroughly involved in overnight ski touring would have a couple different sets of skis. A very light, superfast pair of nordic skis with pin bindings that you can go out and just run on all day and have a great time. And then a pair with Marias edges and Silvretta bindings and big, heavy high-cut boots so you can get up and edge and angulate and carry a pack, and not have such a hard time standing on a narrow platform," says James Jakovec.

Further he suggests that nordic skiers rely on pin bindings and narrow skis, "because they're so much more enjoyable to work with, they conserve energy and track better. They're lighter, and easier to kick and glide with, and you can cover more ground with less expenditure of energy.

"But on the other hand if you're carrying a brutal load and it's rough terrain you can't escape the fact that cable bindings work better than pin bindings, and give you more lateral control. And there are times, frankly, when you just have to edge. And edging, with only 50 cm under the foot, and a heavy pack on your back, is difficult."

A skilled tourer can glide along carrying a pack on skis that are only 49 to 50 cm wide. Paul Kramer, an experienced cross-country skier from Sierra Designs in Berkeley, Calif., advises even beginners to take skis no wider than 55 cm. He acknowledges that it is easier to maneuver through heavy brush and

Ready with the proper clothing and skis for multi-day touring (this photo and those on pages 78, 79 and 83 taken at Sierra Designs, Palo Alto, Calif. Credit-OMPhoto).

edge up hills with wider skis, but insists that on most runs narrow skis are faster. They may give away some time going downhill, but going uphill when you don't have to edge, they "more than make up for it." He also prefers narrower skis because "they're nicer to use skiing around once you get to camp."

They can give fast times. Using light touring skis in the Sierra, Gunnar Vatvedt travelled the 45 miles from Echo Lake to Bear Valley in six hours.

It would also be ideal if your overnight touring skis could be about five centimeters longer than your normal touring ski, says Mike Harding of Mountain Traders, also in Berkeley, Calif. In this case, as with much winter camping equipment, there's a trade-off. Longer skis glide better and shorter skis turn easier.

Paul Kramer warns that American novices buy their skis too long and their poles too short. Norwegians almost never see the need for anything longer than 215s. Only if you are 6'5" and heavy, Paul says, do you need 220s. When you measure poles by standing them under your armpits, make sure the top of the pole fits snugly into the armpit. He suggests the top of the pole should be only 1-1½" below the top of your shoulder.

Jakovec adds, "I don't think I'd go on a multi-night trip with other than an aluminum pole. I wouldn't take a bamboo pole. The potential for it breaking is too great. We break a number of those in our rental program each winter."

The aluminum poles usually cost around $20 (though Eiger Mountain puts out a good one for $14), and bamboo poles run about $7.

Prices should not dissuade you from trying winter camping. Most good mountaineering shops offer a weekend rental package on boots, skis and poles for $8-12. If you already have skis, you'll probably only need to rent a down bag ($5), touring pack which will hug your back ($5), and a two-man mountain tent ($8). So if you have your skis, and can split the fee for a tent with a friend, your equipment costs for a weekend should be under $20.

When choosing boots make sure they have a sole which can readily bend forward but bends very little from side to side. A stiff sole helps your balance on skis. Make sure there's enough room in your boots to move your toes, Paul Kramer says, since movement helps your feet stay warm. The leather should be supple, and yet thick. You should protect against moisture by rubbing in snow seal, but put no snow seal on the sole of your boot if it is made of leather—the oil will soften it and loosen the stitching.

A way to keep your feet warm in very cold weather, Jakovec says, "is to take your oldest pair of rag socks, pull them over your boots, then step into the bindings and lock the bindings down. The snow builds up on the sock rather than the boot. In almost the same way as a snow cave, it acts as an insulator." However, most skiers won't face conditions so severe that they need this protection.

After the trip, your boots should be cleaned off and dried at room temperature.

Taking gaiters along is advisable on every trip, but becomes all the more important on an overnight. Over several days, conditions are more likely to change, and you can't know what you might have to ski through. Gaiters are often needed in the Sierra, where wet and heavy snow is prevalent, but they're not so often needed in the Rockies, where the snow is more likely to be hard, dry and very cold.

There are two schools of thought—one that swears by waterproof gaiters, and the other by breathable ones. Sometimes water will condense inside waterproof gaiters, and sometimes breathable gaiters don't keep the water out. You should experiment for yourself.

You can find gaiters that hook down over your laces, cover your ankle or reach almost to your knees.

Whichever school you join, it's wise to have a waterproof jacket along in case of wet and stormy conditions. A waterproof cagoule cape, which reaches to your ankles and can be either tightened at the wrists or drawn up to free your legs, is good insurance

The clothes you need, like gaiters, depend on the conditions. The standard rule is to dress in layers, not only because this is warmer, but so you can take layers off. As Jakovec says about long underwear, "there are times you can't do without it, and times you hate yourself for putting it on." If you're skiing hard on a still, mild day, you'd best be ready to strip off some layers of clothing. For full mobility you could take off your knickers and put on wind pants over your long underwear, perhaps hiking your wind pants up to the knee. If each leg of your wind pants is a different color, you'll cut quite a figure on the trail.

The type of long underwear you pick is largely a matter of personal choice—whether it's down, polyester, cotton or a combination of cotton and wool.

You can choose between low, medium or high-length gaiters. The medium length is shown here. (OMPhoto)

If you decide to buy, waterproof nylon rain pants cost about $15, and wind pants half as much. Having both along is a good idea.

When it comes to pants, says Jakovec, "knickers are the most preferred. Levis and bellbottoms are the worst because they don't give you the freedom you need in gliding. You burn up energy trying to fight the clothes, and most important, once they're wet they offer no insulation. They should be loose and comfortable, made of one of three materials: down, wool or fiberfill II; and reasonably well put together.

"Still, skiers are notorious for scraping things together. They're like climbers. They just make things work, that's all. I've seen them dressed all the way in full regalia, to bell bottoms and tank tops, so it doesn't matter all that much. The equipment stigma can be too much when people carry tons of lightweight back packing gear."

Your wool knicker socks should come up well over the knee. As Mike Harding reminds us, "there is nothing worse than droopy socks."

The problem with down is that it becomes practically useless when it's wet. Mike Harding recalls a night in January when he was climbing just below Half Dome in Yosemite. It was 18° and they couldn't traverse across the cliff in the dark. No one wanted to lead. Mike leaned back against a rock while they waited, the ice on the rock melted and soaked his jacket. By two o'clock the moon was up and they were moving, but long before that, Mike remembers, his jacket had become a "wet, soggy mass of non-insulating material."

The advantage of wool is that when it's wet, it's still warm. However, when dry it doesn't offer nearly the warmth of down per pound.

The new synthetic materials, such as fiberfill II, weigh somewhat more than down but lose no effectiveness when they get wet. James Jakovec predicts that "when you look at Fiberfill II, you're looking at the next generation of outdoor mountaineering gear. The response to it at North Face has been excellent. The great advantage is that when it does get wet, it retains less than 1% of the water."

Most people warm the top half of their body with a down jacket over several other layers, but there are other combinations . On winter trips Mike Harding wears wool net underwear, a lamb's wool sweater and wool bicycle jersey, and finally, a three-pound wool Dachstein sweater. This is fine in winds up to 10-15 miles per hour. For rougher conditions he adds a nylon cape to break the wind.

He especially recommends the cagoule cape by Swallows Nest for rough weather. It can also be useful, he says, when you're building a snow cave.

It's important to get your down parka and all your upper clothing to reach down over your hips. As a consequence, you might also want your pants somewhat larger in the waist. For most trips, sewn-through down parkas (not the expeditionary style with baffles like a sleeping bag) filled with 8-10 oz. of down are fine.

Well dressed for winter: poplin knickers, wool sweater, down jacket, smile and wool cap. (OMPhoto)

"If the weather is good," Jakovec says, "you can wear virtually any glove on the trail." He also always takes along a pair of Dachstein mittens. "They are my favorite, a heavy, pre-shrunk wool mitten, home woven in Austria—thick and warm. They are the standard for Himalayan expeditions. Get both a comfortable glove and a Dachstein mitten and you can go anywhere you want to go. The way to avoid getting them wet at all is to put a poplin liner over them."

Also, he says: "Using the hood on your jacket is fine, but the problem is that you lose peripheral vision and it's harder to hear. I'm sold on a wool hat, preferably a Balaclava, which is nothing more than a wool helmet. You can pull the whole thing down to the nape of your neck and it's got a place for you to see and a place for you to breathe. They're from Scotland, of long fiber wool, and they've been the standard in expedition work for years."

The Balaclava hats were so named during the Crimean War. British troops wore them under their helmets while fighting near the town of Balaclava, scene of the ill-famed charge of the Light Brigade.

Well dressed, with your skis ready, you pull on your pack. The traditional summer backpack and frame, James Jakovec says, "works well over moderate terrain." It helps if you lower the pack on the frame, or at least put the heavy objects on the bottom of the pack.

But there are specialized ski mountaineering packs that are narrower and cling to your back, some with internal frames. In the past many people found this style of pack to be too short, but now they are being built longer. Some of the better ones are the Ultima-Thule from the Great Pacific Ironworks, Kak-sack from North Face, the Jensen pack from Rivendall, the Palisade Pack from Mountain Traders, and the Kelty tour pack.

"These big, spacious ruck sacks are easier to carry," according to Jakovec. "The idea is to get the center of gravity further down your back, so you'll have more control over your knees and ankles, which determine how smoothly you ski. The idea of good skiing is to keep the upper part of your body motionless, without bouncing and bobbing."

Skiing is definitely more difficult when you're carrying a load, and these packs make it easier. Many good shops rent them.

"At the end of the day," Mike Harding says, "I sit my pack down, take my boots off feet that are probably sweaty, and slip on down booties (2 oz. of down each, ½" Ensolite pad on the bottom) then put on waterproof overboots. Your feet are instantly warm, and this produces a sense of well-being."

Since you're not moontripping, your tent won't pitch itself. If it isn't designed for winter, it may drip, blow down or collapse under a load of snow.

Good winter tents are made of material which breathes, such as 1.9 ripstop nylon. Well-sewn ones have double lines of stitching along the seams, and the fabric is interlocked so there are four layers of material at the seam. Most of the good thread is a cotton and dacron mix.

Also look for catenary cuts—i.e., seams which are arced, instead of being sewn in a straight line. Check along the ridge, and on the seams which come down to the floor. A curved line takes ordinary stretching into account, and will slacken less.

"You have a problem with waterproof tents; if they don't breathe they turn into a steam bath," says James Jakovec. Good tents are made of breathable material but have a waterproof rain fly over the top to keep off moisture. If the fly reaches all the way to the ground it helps the wind from getting un-underneath.

It's easy to drag snow along with you into the tent. "A common trick to is take a kitchen sponge, and cut it in half, and sponge your tent out. Most of the good tents have a cook hole sewn in the bottom, and you can sponge the water back in there," suggests Jakovec. Or you can use a whisk broom.

Most good tent poles are shock cord loaded on the inside, so they will break into pieces but are still connected.

"Some people will use a snow or sand peg. But it still requires that you boot pack, snowshoe pack, or ski pack the spot where you'll pitch the tent. You do that routinely, or the tent is going to sink when you get inside it. Most of the people I know won't go out of their way to carry a sand and snow peg. It's a big ungainly thing about 15 inches long. They look like the front of a shovel, and they're relatively expensive. Except under unusual conditions the pegs which come with the tents won't work at all.

"You're always trying to conserve weight, especially in winter, and the majority of people will use their skis, or snowshoe tails, or poles as anchors. It's more convenient, less expensive, and you're not carrying a multiplicity of things to serve one purpose."

Cooking dinner inside your tent with a gas stove, you'll find that the stoves which work well in summertime (Optimus, Primus, Svea) also work well in winter. Take roughly one-third more fuel than you would take on a summer trip. If you put a 6" square piece of plywood or a three-eighths inch thick piece of Ensolite under the stove, you won't bleed off heat to the ground.

Preparing food and cleaning up is discussed in greater detail on page 57, but the only equipment you really need is two pots, and a bowl and spoon for each person. Cleaning your dishes with snow can be awkward, but if you take some care it might keep you from getting dysentary.

What sort of bag should you slip into at night? Jakovec advises, "A two or two-and-a-half pound down bag is probably sufficient for any problems you'll meet in the Sierra short of full-on mountaineering. Some climbers I know who are making winter ascents using a two-pound bag, sleep in their down jacket. Instead of bringing a big monstrous bag, which few people really need, you can obtain additional warmth by sleeping in your down jacket. You might be adding up to two inches of loft with a down jacket. Usually the two-pound bags are good at temperatures down to zero.

"You've got to insulate the bottom of the bag from the ground or you're going to freeze. One-half inch type M Ensolite is very popular, very efficient, but there seems to be a trend toward comfort. More and more people are going with foam pads—convoluted foam pads, two inches thick, set up with one breatheable surface on top and a waterproof surface on the bottom. Generally you take your clothes into your sleeping bag. Typically the foam pads run hip to shoulder length (either 42" or 54"), since those are the parts of the body that touch the ground first.

"You should put most of your gear in the tent, probably leaving your pack outside the entrance so it's easy to grab in the morning. If you leave your boots outside the tent, they'll freeze just from your perspiration. If you stop and you've got good sunny weather, a common trick is to dry your boots out on the other end of the ski pole that's holding your tent up. Those little goodies, those tricks of the trade, you pick up after numerous mistakes," advises Jakovec.

Washing in the morning is out of the question since you're likely to freeze your face. After dinner, when your metabolism is up, the tent is fairly warm and you're near your bag, is a good time to wash up. After washing you should rub on lanolin or another skin moisturizer. Overnight your body will replace the surface oils which help protect your skin. The humidity in the mountains usually ranges from 5-10%, so the atmosphere dries out your skin. During the day products like Sea and Ski give most people adequate protection in the sun.

If you enjoy winter camping and want your own gear, what can you expect to pay? Mountaineering packs cost from $45 to $65, two-pound down bags from $110-130, tents from $110-160, and down jackets from $40-55.

Increasingly popular three-man hexagonal tent. Rain fly not shown in this photograph. (OMPhoto).

This chapter discusses a plethora of equipment. But you should remember that the natural tendency is to take too much. As James Jakovec says, "There's a direct proportion between your enjoyment of this sport and how little you have to carry."

He adds, "Skiing up to Dewey Point (in Yosemite), stopping and taking some pictures and having a bottle of cold wine and some nice bread and cheese, and skiing back and going to a very warm, comfortable, plush room with hot showers and a temperature of 68 and a half degrees, and then eating a big steak dinner and crashing under an electric blanket—there's a big difference between that and having to bivouac in the middle of a storm and a white-out when everything is wet and you're dog tired and you're not sure if you're really where you want to be."

But the people in the hotel wake up looking at the inside of a building. You'll wake up in a virgin, magical world made new by the night's snowfall.

5

SAFETY

HYPOTHERMIA

BY PAT O'SHEA

A member of the Physical Education staff at Oregon State University in Corvallis, Oregon, Dr. Pat O'Shea has wide experience in outdoor recreation activities such as ski touring, backpacking and winter camping. He has written numerous articles on these activities.

The greatest and most immediate threat to winter campers and other outdoor recreationists is hypothermia, more commonly referred to as exposure in the news media. Hypothermia, by definition, means a lowering of body temperature due to a loss of heat at a rate faster than it can be produced. Below freezing temperatures are not a necessary precondition for hypothermia. Exposure to wet, cold, windy conditions is the most common situation involving hypothermia victims. Physical exhaustion and insufficient food intake are also contributing factors.

In hypothermia, as the central body temperature falls from the normal 98.6°F, various body processes are slowed. Circulation of the blood is retarded, movements become sluggish, coordination is reduced, judgment becomes impaired. With further cooling, unconsciousness results. If the body core temperature drops below 98°F there is increased risk of disorganized heart action or heart stoppage which results in sudden death.

Treatment of hypothermia involves rewarming the body evenly and without delay, but not so rapidly as to further disorganize body functions such as circulation. A hypothermia victim should be immediately protected by all available dry clothing or a sleeping bag and then moved to a warm enclosure. Warm liquids may be given gradually to a conscious person. High, quick energy carbohydrate foods such as candy and honey should be fed but not forced down. Alcohol must never be used in the warming process as it can drive the cold blood from the surface vessels to the body's inner core, thus reducing core temperature.

Defense against hypothermia consists of knowing how and what actions to take to avoid rapid and uncontrolled loss of body heat. To a great extent guarding against hypothermia depends on having a basic understanding of the methods by which the body loses heat and knowing the layer principle of dressing for wilderness travel.

Body heat is lost to the environment through the processes of conduction, convection and radiation. Conduction is the heat exchange between objects at different temperatures when they're in contact with one another. The amount of heat transferred by conduction is proportionate to the temperature difference between the body and the surrounding air—the colder the air the greater the conduction.

Convection is the most important consideration in keeping warm, and wind is the most significant factor here. The human body warms a thin layer of surrounding air by conduction and radiation. However, if the air is being removed by wind convection currents as rapidly as it is warmed up, a high thermal gradient and rate of heat loss will result (see wind chill chart).

Radiation is the transfer of body heat to the surrounding environment. The head is the most critical area in heat loss by radiation. At 40°F, 50% of the body heat is lost through the head and at 5° close to 75%. Remember then, when your feet get cold put your hat on.

Clothing's primary purpose is to interfere with these processes and to assist the body in maintaining thermal equilibrium. Proper clothing, correctly worn, will help the body to adjust to all climatic conditions. In cold weather the clothing does this by holding in the body heat, thereby insulating the body against the outside air. The problem of protection becomes acute when freezing temperatures are involved. Wet clothing must be removed as quickly as possible as it places an additional strain on the heat-producing functions of the body. When backpacking or mountain climbing in freezing temperatures, it

WIND CHILL CHART
Cooling power of wind expressed as "Equivalent Chill Temperature"

Wind (mph)	Actual Air Temperature in °F							
	40	30	20	10	0	-10	-20	-30
5	35	25	15	5	-5	-15	-25	-35
10	30	15	5	-10	-20	-35	-45	-60
15	25	10	-5	-20	-30	-45	-60	-70
20	20	5	-10	-25	-35	-50	-65	-80
25	15	0	-15	-30	-45	-60	-75	-90
30	10	0	-20	-30	-50	-65	-80	-95
35	10	-5	-20	-35	-50	-65	-80	-100
40	10	-5	-20	-35	-55	-70	-85	-100

is imperative to remove and adjust clothing to prevent excessive overheating as it is to add clothing to prevent heat loss.

Cross-country skiing is an active sport and a lot of body heat is generated while skiing. Using several layers of light clothing, instead of one layer of heavy clothing, permits the skier to adjust for various activity levels and temperature conditions. If one perspires heavily while skiing, the insulation value of the clothing is reduced. Wet undershirts should be removed, and replaced with dry clothing.

Clothing must serve as an insulator for the thin layer of warm air surrounding the body. Wool clothing is an excellent insulator (even when wet, 70% of its insulating qualities are retained) since it contains within its fibers thousands of tiny air pockets. These air pockets trap the air warmed by the body and hold it close to the skin. The principle of trapping air within the

"Cross-country skiing is an active sport and a lot of body heat is generated while skiing. Using several layers of light clothing, instead of one layer of heavy clothing, permits the skier to adjust for various activity levels and temperature conditions. (Miles Becker photo)

Ed Park photo

fibers or layers of clothing provides the most efficient method of insulating the body against heat loss.

Cotton, nylon or rayon clothing has little or none of the insulating qualities of wool, down or dacron. Remember that when down becomes wet it is useless as an insulator. To be an effective insulator, down items (clothing and sleeping bags) must be kept dry. This is a major problem in a hard, wind-driven rain.

In dressing for wilderness travel, the layers of clothing used are of different design and material. Underwear is porous or may be of the fishnet design with air space insulation for warmth. Over the underwear is a cotton T-shirt to absorb perspiration. Next, a light wool shirt covered by either a heavy wool sweater or a down vest. Down is breathable, allowing body moisture to escape freely, and provides great warmth over an extremely wide range of temperatures..

A quality parka is made of 60/40 cloth (60% cotton, 40% nylon). The cotton absorbs body perspiration very quickly while the nylon provides the strength and abrasion resistance to wear.

For leg protection in cold weather, wear fishnet underwear beneath wool pants. Also carry along a pair of waterproof nylon rain pants in your pack for emergency use.

A waterproof outer shell, while giving protection from rain and moisture, does not allow air to circulate and the body perspiration to escape. Instead, the perspiration fills the airspaces of the inside clothing with moisture-laden air and reduces their insulating qualities. In this situation, unless the wet clothing can be dried or emergency clothing is available, a serious problem has developed. Stopping to rest in sub-freezing temperatures in this condition will most likely result in hypothermia.

If you keep in mind the idea that when you're actively skiing you need much less insulation than when resting, the following chart prepared by the

US Army Quartermaster can be a valuable aid. The chart gives a rough approximation of the thickness of insulation required for safety and comfort. The temperature that is given is the effective air temperature without wind. Numerous other factors, however, affect our response to cold. Among these are the relative humidity, altitude, physical condition, type and quantity of food intake, emotional state, and the rate of metabolism (the amount and intensity of physical work being done).

Insulation thickness required at various temperatures

Effective Temperature	Sleeping	Light Work	Heavy Work
40°F	1.5"	.8"	.20"
20°F	2.0"	1.0"	.27"
0°F	2.5"	1.3"	.35"
–20°F	3.0"	1.6"	.40"
–40°F	3.5"	1.9"	.48"
–60°F	4.0"	2.1"	.52"

AVOIDING HAZARDS

BY LARRY MOITOZO

Larry Moitozo has hiked, climbed, backpacked, cross-country skied and kayaked from Hawaii to Switzerland. He's a certified cross-country ski instructor, developed the Youth Science Institute wilderness program in California, and teaches a wilderness ecology summer course at the University of California in Santa Cruz. He has extensive experience in the California Sierra (including several winter trans-Sierra trips), the Cascades, the Rocky Mountains and Alaska. For the past 20 years he has spent every summer in one or more of the above wilderness areas.

There's an old Irish saying (or proverb) that, repeated properly, is supposed to protect you from "wilderness beasties, and long-legged creatures that go 'BUMP' in the night". While I have no doubt as to the effectiveness of this procedure, I'd like to deal a bit more directly with the "wilderness beasties."

The wilderness both in winter and summer is really a safe place. If, however, you're in an accident in the wilderness, it may be very difficult to get assistance. Other sections of this book will duplicate in one way or another some of the things I have included here, but because of the obvious advantage of avoiding hazards it is worthwhile (even at the risk of some duplication) to become thoroughly familiar with these "wilderness beasties."

Accidents usually catch you unaware, or are apt to happen when your awareness is, at least, diverted. The American Alpine Club's publication on mountaineering accidents is literally filled with incidents that affirm this. Something relatively unimportant happens—say, a lost glove leads to a painfully cold hand. The leader, attempting to select a more protected route, leads the group into an avalanche path. So the suggestion is to watch out for the little things. Make changes from known, proven, and safe procedures only after very careful considerations. Check out new ideas with other members of the group. Sometimes just verbalizing what you have in mind will reveal to you the folly of it all and revitalize your own awareness.

AVALANCHE SAFETY

Avalanches are the most famous, or infamous, of all winter wilderness hazards. Dave Beck's article "Better Safe Than Buried" (page 103) gives complete details on avalanche safety. In short, avoid crossing in front of potential avalanches but if you must cross them, cross as high as possible—and one person at a time. Read the section on avalanche safety for the exact procedure on crossing.

In a near-tragic personal event, a group of us were fun racing up the leeward side of a ridge. The first to the top was to be rewarded with the excellent view. He was rewarded, all right—with a clattering 40-foot cold, wet and snowy drop. He had skied out onto the top of a cornice that was impossible to see from the top of the ridge. Needless to say, we all approach ridges very carefully now.

TENT FIRES

A hazard which until recently was often overlooked in winter camping literature is that of tent fires. Almost every item used in a mountaineering tent is flammable, including the tent itself! Nylon burns readily and so does dacron, particularly the type used as insulation. Open flames of all sorts should be avoided inside tents. Candles without protective lanterns can turn a tent into a flaming holocaust by simply turning over and igniting a dacron insulated garment.

If you must cook inside of a tent, use extreme caution. Always support the pot when stirring its contents. Prime the stove carefully and caution the tent occupants when you're doing this so they won't flip a nylon sleeve or sleeping bag into the open flame. Also, do not over-fill your white gasoline stove so that the pressure valve is covered by gasoline. If the valve should allow excess pressure to escape, it will also shoot out the excess gasoline. The result can be a pretty good imitation of a small flame thrower.

Caution is mandatory in refueling stoves. Make certain the stove is cool. A hot stove can cause spilled fuel to become explosive. Mere contact between fuel and a candle flame or smoking materials (pipe, cigarette, etc.) can cause an explosion. Fuel spilled onto clothing can increase the flammability of the garment to create an extreme hazard. Fires in tents happen very quickly! When they happen, the least one can expect is a ruined tent; the worst is too terrible to contemplate. So be careful with fires, stoves and fuel around tents.

GETTING LOST

Getting lost is one of the hazards to avoid when travelling through the wilderness. Take care neither you nor anyone else in your party gets lost. Make certain everybody on the trip knows the destination. Because we are all different and have different physical capabilities, it is often difficult for all members of a party to ski or snowshoe at the same rate.

If you find the same person in the party is always in the rear when periodic stops are made, try lightening that person's load, letting some of the faster travellers take on more weight.

Above all, don't rest for 10 minutes and take off as soon as the "slowpoke" shows up. This person may be really the one who needs the rest most, not you "speedsters" who got there first. Find out what his problem is (without putting him down) and relieve the problem if you can. Remember that some people merely prefer to go slower. But check this out with the person and keep an eye out for him.

MAP AND COMPASS

Particularly on extensive trips, make certain you know how to use a map and compass. There are often no reliable trails to follow. While you may

Expedition to Alaska's remote Brooks Mountain Range. The success of such an expedition depends on knowing what to expect in the winter wilderness. (Jack Miller photo)

be thoroughly familiar with the summer topography of an area, snow in winter may throw your familiar landmarks way off. The foot paths are gone, hidden under feet of snow, and so might be the familiar log crossings and sign posts. Winter air is often clearer and the light conditions (ask any photographer) often distort distances to an incredible degree.

Check the distances travelled carefully. Get some idea of how fast your group is travelling. Even on the flat, an inexperienced group, particularly if heavily loaded, may be going only a mile an hour. All these elements and many more tend to influence your calculations with map and compass.

LOSING EQUIPMENT ITEMS

Losing equipment is often one of those little things that lead to bigger and worse accidents. Losing a ski or a part of a ski is one of those "little things." Skiers often jamb the tails of their skis into the snow so the skis will stand upright overnight. A camper stumbling out on a nature's night trip can easily fall over a ski in the dark and break off the tail. While you can carry a spare ski tip, I've never heard of a spare ski tail! You might possibly be able to tape the tail back together, but it's much simpler to put your skis where they'll be safe in the first place.

I generally put my skis out of the general traffic pattern around a tent area. I make sure they won't be broken by securing the ski poles in the snow, then putting the tips through the handle straps. Then if that night tripper comes by, he will only knock the ski over. In the morning I can usually tell where it is, even if it's been snowing, because I always put the other ski only six feet or so away.

Incidentally, before you begin a trip examine your bindings—if you're using skis. It's a lot easier to tighten a screw or reset the bale in its socket than to remount the binding after it has pulled out. A bale lost in the soft snow is also very hard to find. It it's a large bale, try using your compass. Sometimes the steel will divert the needle if you get close enough to it.

It's also a potentially hazardous practice to use ski poles and skis for tent pegs. The tails of the skis can be broken off, or at least damaged so that the ski starts to delaminate. And the basket (if the poles are used tip down) can come off when you try to pull the pole out of the frozen snow in the morning. If you put the pole in the snow handle down, you face an even more serious problem: the tip can gouge or injure someone.

In case you lose your gloves, you can usually compensate by substituting wool socks. However, the lack of a thumb slot (with socks) quickly demonstrates the extreme facility of the human thumb. I've seen people "driven crazy" to such an extent by the lack of a thumb piece that they have slit the sock and stitched in a thumb piece.

SNOW-BLINDNESS

Lost sunglasses usually require a bit more ingenuity than lost gloves. It's important to understand that snow-blindness doesn't hurt to get—only to have. In other words, the pain is the result of the damage.

When you have snow-blindness, it feels like sand under your eyelids and seeing is difficult. Protection after you get it does not relieve the symptoms; it only prevents further damage. So even if the person who has lost his glasses doesn't complain, make him or her wear emergency devices anyway.

Eskimo glasses are an answer. They can be made in a variety of ways. They are mainly slits, cut in some material, that allow only a band of light to enter the eye. Cardboard and string, or a bandanna tied "desperado fashion" with slits over the eyes are but two ways to make your own Eskimo glasses. I'll bet that you can come up with a dozen better ways.

Obviously, when dealing with equipment, it's infinitely easier to organize your pack and equipment in such a fashion as to minimize losses than to be forced to "fake it" with a make-shift system. Besides, it avoids those little situations which often lead to bigger ones.

THE DANGER OF GETTING WET

Getting either yourself or your equipment soaking wet can also lead to serious trouble. When getting yourself wet is combined with inadequate or improper clothing, the road to trouble is considerably shortened. For example, tight-fitting cotton jeans can act as a heat sink or backwards radiation to a human body.

You get wet in a variety of ways on the trail. The most common ways are: continuous falling into wet or damp snow; over-exertion; and falling into streams or ponds. If proper clothing is used (wet wool insulates almost

as well as dry cotton), the effect of the falling problem can be minimized. The "layer principle" of clothing can also relieve the perspiration problem in over-exertion (you wear fewer layers when you're more active). Finally, in crossing streams or getting water out of them, the necessary care and a little ingenuity should keep you from falling in.

Should you get wet for some reason, it's important, as stated elsewhere in this book, to get dry as quickly as possible and before your internal body temperature decreases. As you probably know, when the temperature of the body's inner core drops the condition is called hypothermia. If steps aren't taken to prevent any further heat loss and then to re-heat the hypothermia victim, he may die.

It should be noted that the skin can be quite cold for quite a period of time before hypothermia occurs (depending on the temperature of the air). The reason for this is that the circulatory system of the body goes into a "shunting" process to help sustain the core temperature. In this process blood is allowed to flow directly from the arterioles into the venioles without going through the capillaries near the skin surface.

Obviously, once the shunt system begins to operate in an area of severe heat loss the blood supply to that surface area is curtailed. In order to re-open the blood flow to the capillaries an outside heat source is needed. But care must be taken in re-warming an area, too. The effect of cold on the skin is to render the sensors in the skin less reliable. Under certain conditions there will be more sensation than normal and under different conditions less sensation. At any rate, there is enough variability so the reactions of the cold individual cannot be taken as accurate. Therefore, care must be taken not to further injure cold skin.

After all is said and done, though, the things we have talked about here are really all part of the great exciting game. "What game?" you ask. Well, that of facing the "wilderness beasties and long-legged creatures that go 'BUMP' in the night"—and coming away smiling, of course.

FIRST AID AND EMERGENCY

BY GALE GREGORY

A *Nordic World* contributor, Gale Gregory is an experienced cross-country skier and has participated in several winter rescues.

Going into the winter wilderness requires somewhat more planning and flexibility than going into the same terrain in summer or spring. Ideally, every group of winter campers should have an experienced leader who is well prepared to handle any situation that may arise. A situation which would merely be uncomfortable in warm weather can turn into a real disaster in sub-freezing temperatures. Beforehand knowledge of what can lie ahead and how to handle emergencies is the most important information you can take with you on any type of winter trip.

Safety gear is an integral part of winter camping equipment. Many items double up and are used for different purposes, many others can be converted from summer use into winter use, and still others are highly specialized; but none should ever be left behind. The following list is a good starting place for a party of four embarking on an overnight camping trip on skis or snowshoes.

● *Matches*—Most winter campers have discovered that using a butane or white gas stove is far superior to a fire in every way except aesthetically. With the vanishing supply of deadwood in most travelled wilderness areas, this is sound practice ecologically as well as a matter of convenience. However, in an emergency, a fire must often be built to dry wet clothing (and skiers) or to provide warmth for an injured person. Windproof, waterproof outdoor matches can be purchased at most sporting goods stores, and a supply should be carried by each member of the party.

● *Space Brand Rescue Blanket*—Every skier should also carry one of these little gems. They are lightweight, cheap, strong and will reflect up to 80% of the body's heat when wrapped and tucked around a person. They can only be used once, however, so be sure to replace any that are worn.

● *Whistle*—One whistle should suffice for a party of four, unless the plans include splitting up. Three short blasts on a good police whistle will carry for miles and is the universally recognized distress signal.

● *Plastic or aluminum ski tip*—Again, one should be adequate for a group of four. Be certain, however, that the ski tip is of the correct size to fit each skier's skis. They come in several widths and styles. A ski with a broken tip is worse than useless—unless you know how to repair it—and the attachable tip will allow the accident victim to arrive at his destination relatively unfrustrated.

● *Combination tool*—This writer's personal choice is a combination knife, screwdriver, pick, wrench and file. This tool goes everywhere I do, city or country, and has proven itself invaluable. The wrench end can also be used as a light hammer when necessary.

● *Small package of screws, nails, safety pins*—"For want of a nail..." Screws and things *do* pop loose from bindings, frame packs, stoves and other equipment. Being able to replace them on the spot can save aborting a trip. Electricians black tape is also a very useful repair item, and is vital if you have to repair bamboo ski poles.

Nylon cord, good sunglasses or goggles, sunburn cream, toilet paper, a wool hat or balaclava, dry socks and glove liners aren't normally thought of as safety gear, but are very necessary and can prevent a good deal of discomfort.

FIRST-AID KIT

Also along on every overnight trip should be a fairly complete first-aid kit. Most kits sold in stores are not worth the bother to buy or carry. You can assemble a far better one yourself with a little help from your doctor. Completed, it will weight less than a pound and should handle any type of medical emergency until professional help can be reached. You can take this kit on camping trips all year around, but, of course, you won't need a snake-bite kit or poison oak lotion in winter.

Your first-aid kit should include the following:

Band-aids—10 of them, 1" wide, for blisters, scratches, etc.

Butterfly Closures—10, medium size, for cuts and lacerations that don't require sutures.

Sterile Gauze Pads—six, 4" x 4" for dressing wounds and to use as compresses to stop bleeding.

Eye pads—two, for eye injuries and snow-blindness.

Roller Gauze—one package, 2" wide, for dressing wounds and holding splints.

Adhesive Tape—1" wide, at least five yards.

Ace Bandage—4" wide, for support, splints, sprains.

Aluminum Finger Splint—Broken fingers are a fairly common outdoor occurence.

Neosporin Ointment—One of the most common outdoor injuries in winter is the first or second degree burn. Fingers are always being poked too close to stoves and fires. The best treatment for small-area burns is plunging the injured part in ice water for a few minutes. In the winter camping situation, however, frostbite is an ever-present danger, so do not overdo this treatment. Coat the burn with ointment, and bandage loosely.

Aspirin and Codeine—20 aspirin tablets and 10 ½-gram codeine tablets for relief of pain (stomach upsets, for instance, intensify with increasing altitude). Ask your doctor for the codeine to be prescribed separately, in case it must be given to someone with an aspirin sensitivity.

Antibiotics—As prescribed by a physician, antibiotics can be used to combat infection. These drugs are not usually needed on overnight trips, but should be carried on longer journeys. It is important to know that any antibiotic should not be taken just once or twice. The course of treatment must be contineud for at least three days if the infection is not to re-occur.

Garamycin Eye Solution— Useful for any eye injury or snow blindness. Use in affected eye three or four times daily and keep the eye bandaged.

(**Note**: Some of these drugs require a doctor's prescription and should be used with his guidance.)

The above kit can handle most medical emergencies on a winter camping trip. Of course, each member of the party should be sure to bring his or her own medical needs, such as insulin, birth control pills, etc. Tranquilizers and sedatives are rarely needed in the outdoors. Healthy exercise, fresh air and the silence of the winter outdoors provides all the relaxation necessary for a good night's sleep.

INJURIES

Every winter camper should have a working knowledge of elementary first aid and self help.

Most skiers and winter campers will have a nodding acquaintance with frostbite sooner or later and it is wise to always be on the lookout for its symptoms. Only the mildest cases of superficial "frost-nip" can be treated in the field. Any case of frostbite is potentially serious and should be handled as such. The first symptoms include a blanching or paling of the skin, followed by a loss of the feeling of cold and discomfort. The affected part should be warmed immediately (Never, never rub the frozen area with snow. Following this old wives' tale will only increase the permanent tissue damage.) Fingers and toes can be held in the armpits or groin. Earlobes should be held by warm hands. Nose tips should be warmed and covered.

Cases of deep frostbite must be evacuated before rewarming occurs. You can walk a long way on frozen toes or feet with very little additional damage, but once the frozen parts have been thawed, the victim must be immobilized. Proper care of frostbite patients cannot be maintained in camp, but fortunately deep frostbite is quite rare in properly equipped and experienced ski parties.

Leg fractures in cross-country skiing are extremely rare. If one should occur, splint the leg according to standard first-aid practice and evacuate the victim. In the National Parks, rangers usually have the capabilities for winter evacuation. In National Forests, the county sheriff usually does this job, and if you're close to a ski area the National Ski Patrols are a potential source of assistance.

It is important *not* to leave an injured person alone. Broken bones are painful and the victim usually cannot care for himself. If you *must* leave the victim (because of the size of your party—two people, for example) make certain the victim has water, is warm, etc. Never leave a victim if he is in shock or unconscious. Invariably when this has been done, the victim has died.

Mountain sickness is a malaise that the wilderness skier gets from going too high too fast. It isn't serious, and can be cured rapidly by descending to lower altitude, or resting for a day or two at whatever height the sufferer started feeling sick. Symptoms vary from nausea, headaches, loss of appetite, apathy, shortness of breath or just feeling plain rotten. Most people aren't affected until they reach 8000 feet or higher, but it can hit at much lower altitudes than that. It is important to know that a skier with the mountain miseries should not force himself onward and upward, but rest until the symptoms disappear.

IN CASE OF STORM

Eventually, every touring skier and winter camper will be faced with an unexpected change in the weather when out on a trip. A warm and sunny afternoon can suddenly turn into a dark and stormy night in a matter of minutes. The properly equipped ski party, armed with the knowledge to make the correct decision under emergency weather conditions, need have no fear about changing a possible hazard into several months worth of cocktail party conversation. Decisions must be made immediately, and a good rule of thumb to follow is: when in doubt, wait it out.   More skiers and winter hikers have been lost and injured because they attempted to travel during adverse weather conditions than almost any other reason.

Of course, each particular circumstance is different and should be judged on its own merits. If your party is within a mile of the road, you have some visibility and the trail is marked, it makes more sense to push on through a storm than wait. But if there is any doubt at all as to the direction to take, it is far wiser to set up an unexpected camp and "hole in" until the skies clear. Every overnight ski party should *always* have additional food along for an emergency camp. One meat bar per person, a few chocolate bars, space food sticks or some extra cheese will provide the necessary warmth and energy to make an unplanned night out an inconvenience, not a tragedy.

Properly equipped and planned, winter camping trips are an exhilarating experience every outdoors person can learn to love. Placing the right emphasis on good, sound, safe procedures, learning not to exceed your own limits and capabilities, and enjoying the silent solitude of forests and mountains in winter can be one of the most richly rewarding adventures of a lifetime.

BETTER SAFE THAN BURIED

BY DAVE BECK

Snow is a large part of a ski-tourer's and winter camper's environment. He skis on it. He may melt it for water. He may make a shelter from it in the form of an igloo or a snow cave. And, if he is not careful, he may be buried by a snow avalanche. Some knowledge of the processes occurring within a snowpack is necessary for the winter camper who wants to build a snow cave or pick a safe route through avalanche country.

SNOW METAMORPHISM

Snow is always evolving, or metamorphosing. There are three types of snow metamorphism: equitemperature metamorphism, temperature-gradient metamorphism, and melt metamorphism (also called firnification). Temperature determines which type of metamorphism snow will undergo. Temperature-gradient metamorphism occurs during the coldest months and firnification during the warmer spring months.

During the winter months equitemperature metamorphism is the most common type. It occurs when new snow loses its original (crystalline) form in a process called sublimation. In sublimation, water molecules are released from ice as water vapor and then the vapor molecules are redeposited as ice molecules on some cold surface. The rate of the process depends on the air temperature. Sublimation takes place at a much faster rate as the temperature rises.

One important aspect of equitemperature metamorphism is snowpack settlement. When the snow crystals lose their original shape, changing to small grains, the entire snowpack shrinks and settles. Settling snow is one indication of a stable pack that is not likely to avalanche.

Another type of metamorphism is called temperature gradient metamorphism. It is not as common along warmer coastal ranges as in colder places, such as Alaska and Colorado. It requires loose snow and a temperature difference, or gradient, in the snowpack, the coldest section of the snow being nearest the surface.

Snow is a good radiator of infrared (long-wave) radiation. During early winter, a snowpack may lose more heat than it gains. When the sun is low and there is no warm wind, the snowpack's surface temperature lowers as the snow gives off long-wave radiation. A snowpack will also lose heat from its surface rapidly if there are very cold clouds overhead.

In temperature-gradient metamorphism, the subliming water vapor migrates upward in the snow and, when it solidifies, forms a unique type of crystal called depth hoar (or sugar snow).

One of the best ways to detect temperature-gradient metamorphism is to push a ski pole into the snow. If there is less resistance close to the ground, you should suspect that temperature-gradient metamorphism has taken place.

The changes that are induced by alternate thawing and refreezing are called melt metamorphism. When some surface snow melts, water percolates down through the layers of snow, melts the bonds between snow grains and converts the snow into a loose, wet mass, which may avalanche. Once refrozen, however, the snowpack is stronger than before. The grains are larger and better bonded because they have been coated with meltwater and refrozen.

During early winter, some melt metamorphism will occur on lower sunny slopes. A thin layer of the snow surface will melt during the day and then freeze at night, forming a thin, breakable sun crust.

As spring progresses, melt metamorphism takes place faster. Often the snow surface is too soft and slushy to ski on in the afternoon. Sometimes during April there is a period (the spring thaw) of a few days or weeks when an entire snowpack reaches a temperature of 32°. When night temperatures do not drop below freezing, one should suspect that the pack is thawing. The spring thaw is very dangerous. The thaw, of course, occurs at different times in different regions. Newly wet, unbonded snow is likely to avalanche, particularly if there are any weak layers within the pack. Since melt metamorphism is a stabilizing process, the danger of spring avalanches is less after a snowpack has thawed and refrozen a few times; the pack will have settled and become well bonded.

Melt metamorphism takes place every time it rains. While wet, the snowpack is unstable. In fact, a heavy rainstorm can rapidly change a stable, well-bonded pack into a dangerous loose, wet mass of snow which will flow like mud.

AVALANCHES

Snow is a surprisingly complex substance. It can stretch like a rubber band—and snap like one—or it can flow sluggishly like molasses. A snowpack that supported hundreds of skiers in the morning may warm and avalanche under one skier in the afternoon. So many variables affect a snowpack that any generalization about snow and avalanches must have numerous exceptions. Consequently, evaluating an avalanche hazard is difficult.

A slab avalanche occurs when a whole mass of snow slides, leaving a fracture line at the upper part of the slide path where the slab has broken loose. A slab avalanche is characterized as soft or hard. To tell which, note whether the debris is in recognizable blocks after the avalanche has come to rest. If blocks are evident, it's a hard-slab avalanche. If the debris is in one mass, it's a soft-slab avalanche. The dividing line between the two types is hazy.

A loose-snow, or point, avalanche starts at a point and becomes wider and larger as it moves downhill. A loose-snow avalanche looks like a large fan.

A slab or a loose-snow avalanche may be dry, damp or wet. If the snow in it contains visible water, it is wet. If you can't see water but can make a snowball, it is damp. If the snow is not cohesive enough to form a snowball, it is dry.

The immediate cause of an avalanche is known as an avalanche trigger. Snow falling from a tree or a cornice, new snow piling up, or a careless skier—all can be avalanche triggers. Most of the avalanches in which skiers are involved are triggered by the skiers themselves. Perhaps the one rule about avalanches to which there are no exceptions is: *Never ski, snowshoe, camp or walk in a spot where you may trigger an avalanche.*

EVALUATING AN AVALANCHE HAZARD

Snow rangers evaluate an avalanche hazard according to the following 10 conditions (the order of importance of these conditions is different for different storms):

1. Depth of old snow. Deep snow increases the hazard by covering small obstructions and smoothing out avalanche paths. Small bushes, rock, and irregularities of the terrain help prevent avalanches by anchoring the snowpack to the ground. And since a more uneven surface needs a deeper snowpack to cover it, some slopes are not dangerous unless the snow is deep. Other slopes, such as smooth, grassy hillsides, are dangerous when only a few inches of snow are on the ground.

2. Condition of old snow. If there are any weak layers of snow within a a snowpack, an avalanche is more likely. Layers that have undergone temperature-gradient metamorphism are particularly dangerous. Buried ice layers are impermeable to water. Rainwater or meltwater will flow on the surface of a buried ice layer and melt some of the snow above it; if too much snow melts, all the snow above this ice layer will avalanche.

3. New-snow depth. The deeper the new snow (other things being equal), the higher the avalanche hazard.

4. New-snow type. Very small crystals, such as needles, or very large crystals, such as graupel, tend to cause avalanches—especially slab avalanches—because they form dense snow. Stellar and plate crystals usually do not form slab avalanches unless there are high winds.

5. Snowfall intensity. The rate of snowfall, measured in inches per hour, is an indication of avalanche potential. One inch per hour is dangerous. Four inches per hour is a very high and hazardous rate.

6. Precipitation intensity. During rains and during snowfalls of dense snow crystals the precipitation intensity may be very high even though the snowfall intensity is not. Precipitation intensity is measured in inches of water per hour. An intensity greater than .10 inch per hour is hazardous. The longer the rate stays high, the greater the avalanche hazard.

7. Snow settlement. Snow that is settling is relieving inner stresses; it is becoming more stable. Hence snow settlement is a good way to measure avalanche hazard; as the snow settles, the hazard lessens.

8. Temperature. If the air is warm, a snowpack settles more rapidly. The colder it is, therefore, the longer the avalanche hazard lasts.

During early winter, the snow surface cools, thus helping bring about temperature-gradient metamorphism. Later in the winter, warmer temperatures speed snow settlement. However, very warm temperatures melt snow on on the surface and eventually make the whole snowpack wet, destroying all the bonds between the snow grains and raising the probability of wet avalanches. The longer the above-freezing period—the spring thaw—lasts, the higher the avalanche hazard becomes. If there are no weak snow layers, the avalanches that occur will likely involve surface layers only. But if the snow has weak layers within it, look for large avalanches. The thaw will often be interrupted, and the hazard lessened, after a few nights by subfreezing temperatures.

Any change of temperature from cold to near 32° should be considered hazardous. During spring, the temperature will rapidly rise after a cold storm (snow below 32° F). The avalanche hazard will persist for several days, until the new snow completely undergoes melt metamorphism.

9. **Wind.** The most common type of avalanche in Colorado is the hard slab. During the cold Colorado winters, wind packs snow crystals into dense slabs. The slabs do not settle, but remain poised like giant, fragile, irregular arches.

The most common avalanches in California, on the other hand, are soft slabs. Typically, they are soft wind slabs that take place during storms. Any wind can pack snow together to make a slab. High winds (above 15 miles an hour) are dangerous because they pack the wind slabs together so tightly that the snow load will get very large before it avalanches.

10. **New-snow density.** The more dense a layer of new snow is, the higher the avalanche hazard. Most of the snow that falls in California has a density of near .10 g/cm^3; in other words, it is about 10% water. Very dry new snow contains as little as 4% water; very wet new snow has as much as 40% water.

AVALANCHE PATHS

Obviously one should never camp in an avalanche path. A competent outdoorsman, even when he is sure that there is no hazard, still feels uncomfortable in an avalanche path.

In a timbered region, avalanche paths that cut swaths straight down the mountainside through timber are common sights. Often an avalanche will top a tree or strip branches (avalanche burn) from the uphill side of a tree. It is always interesting to study an avalanche path that slides only once every 10 or 20 years. Such a path contains an even-aged stand of young trees. The height of topped trees tells where the sliding surface of an avalanche was.

Most avalanches that are dangerous originate on slopes of between 25° and 60°. However, under exceptional circumstances (e.g., during heavy rains) slopes as gentle as 10° can avalanche. For a large avalanche to occur, snow must stick to a hillside long enough to accumulate into a mass. On very steep hillsides snow constantly sluffs, never piling up deep enough to cause an avalanche. Sluffs continually falling down a steep hillside will either trigger avalanches or stabilize lower slopes. On slopes steeper than 60°, high winds can form slabs that won't avalanche until a large mass of snow has accumulated. It is dangerous, however, to estimate avalanche hazard by slope alone. There are too many variables—e.g., wind, temperature, and snowfall intensity. Any slope above 25° should be considered dangerous.

The shape of a slope and the ground cover on it influence avalanches. Convex slopes are more dangerous than concave ones. A dense stand of timber will retard slab avalanches, but loose avalanches will flow right through timber. All that the existence of an open stand of timber assures one is that any avalanches that passed through the trees were not large enough to damage them. Often a fracture line in the snow will run from the edge of a cliff along the middle of a convex slope to a tree or another cliff. Large trees can help stabilize the lower layers of a snowpack which would otherwise be unstable. A smooth surface like a granite slab or a grassy slope is an excellent sliding surface for an avalanche.

According to Forest Service data, half the people who are buried in avalanches die within one hour. It is obvious that a skier who is buried has little chance of surviving if not quickly found.

One should, of course, avoid being in a place where an avalanche can occur. This rule is easy to state, but it is not always easy to follow. There are situations in which the winter outdoorsman, because of poor route-finding, ignorance or some other reason, will find himself on an avalanche path. When that happens the following rules should be followed:

● Use an avalanche cord. There is some feeling against avalanche cords because they become tangled in ski poles, tree trunks, etc., but they have saved lives. With practice you can learn to ski with one. Use a bright-colored, lightweight nylon cord at least 50 feet long. One end should be tied securely around the waist, the other end trailing behind.

● Remove the straps of the ski poles from your wrists. Unfasten safety, or arlberg, straps when skiing in an avalanche path; tuck them into the tops of your gaiters. Unfasten the waist belt of your pack.

● If the snow is not too soft, take off your skis and walk across the avalanche path. Pick the safest route by taking advantage of trees, cliffs, and ledges.

● Cross the avalanche path one person at a time. All other members of the party should watch the crossing skier. The party should not ski on until the last person has crossed.

It is possible to ski out of a small avalanche if you are near its side and it is not going too fast (some avalanches have been clocked at 250 miles an hour).

If you are caught in an avalanche, try to take off your skis or snowshoes and rid yourself of poles and pack. Often there will not be time, but you should try.

After ridding yourself of all gear, attempt a backstroke in the flowing snow so that you will plane closer to the surface. Just before the avalanche stops, lunge upward. In a large, turbulent avalanche, however, you will be so tumbled and tossed about that you will lose all sense of direction. Then all you can do is protect your face with one arm, to help provide an air space around your face and to keep you from inhaling snow. Put your other arm out at a right angle to your body; it may stick out of the snow. A buried skier can only hope that his fellow tourers find him.

AVALANCHE RESCUE

Those who see an avalanche bury a skier should note very carefully the exact point where the skier was caught and last seen. A victim's location is never certain, since the pattern of turbulence within flowing snow cannot be known exactly, but the victim will likely be buried somewhere down the fall line from the point where he was last seen. (The fall line is the path of least resistance downward from a point—the path a rolling snowball would follow) With their skis off, rescuers should search down the fall line below the point where the victim was last seen on the avalanche path. Search around all likely burial points, such as the uphill sides of trees, the outsides of bends in the avalanche path, and the bases of cliffs. If you find anything the victim was wearing or carrying, leave it in place and mark it with a ski pole. Its location helps determine the line in which the victim was carried.

A thorough search should be made down the fan-shaped area extending from the last-seen point to the foot of the avalanche. If you cannot find the buried skier by carefully searching the surface of the debris, you will have to probe. Probing by a small party is almost never successful because it takes too long. Half the victims buried three feet deep in an avalanche die within 45 minutes; half of those buried two feet deep die within 75 minutes; and half of those buried one foot deep die within 105 minutes. Near ski resorts, where rescue equipment and trained personnel are available, probing can be effective. But on a ski tour or winter camping trip, where help may be hours away, a buried person is in serious trouble if probing is the only method of finding him.

There are two methods of probing. In *coarse probing* the rescuers stand side-by-side, about 10 inches apart. Everyone probes once in front of himself. Then the line advances 24 inches and everyone probes again. *Fine probing* is much more thorough and slower. The rescuers stand almost shoulder-to-shoulder. Everyone probes by his left foot, in front of himself, and then by his right foot. Then the rescuers advance 12 inches and repeat the probing. A probe line must be carefully maintained if the searchers are not to miss any portion of the avalanche debris. Coarse probing is about five times as fast as fine probing, and since time is so important in avalanche rescue, coarse probing is more likely to be successful.

Collapsible 10-foot avalanche probes, which weigh only a few pounds, should be carried on trips in avalanche areas. Skis can be used, but they do not work well in debris from wet avalanches and won't probe deeper than four or five feet. A lightweight snow shovel is also handy in an avalanche rescue.

Once a victim has been located and dug out, the first thing to check is his breathing. If it has stopped, one person should begin mouth-to-mough artificial respiration immediately. Meanwhile, other party members should wrap the victim in spare clothing to keep him warm. Once his breathing has been restored, he should be examined carefully for broken bones and other injuries. Remember that an avalanche victim is always in shock, and treat him accordingly.

Much time and energy have been devoted to inventing a device that would locate avalanche victims. In Europe, carefully trained dogs are used to find buried skiers, but in North America, surface searching and probing are now the only ways to locate a victim, unless he is wearing some special device such as the Skadi. This is a radio that transmits and receives signals, through any substance, across a distance of 100 feet. Since 1969 the Skadi has been used by many ski patrols, Forest Service snow rangers, and others who work where avalanches occur. Swiss studies have shown that one person with a Skadi can search a large area in the same time that 600 well-organized probers can. It has already saved lives in Canada. The one drawback for a part-time skier or winter camper is Skadi's price: between $105 and $135 each, depending on how many you buy (each member of a touring party should carry one). Information about the device can be obtained from Monty Atwater, 11 Cloudview Trail, Sausalito, California 94965.

6

ADVENTURE

SIERRA CROSSING

BY PAUL EMERSON

The ultimate winter camping experience is an expedition or a multi-day adventure trip. This article is about such a trip—a nine-day snowshoe crossing of the Sierra Nevada the author made last winter with two companions. An avid mountaineer, Paul Emerson is a newspaperman by profession (arts editor of the Palo Alto Times in Palo Alto, California).

The idea of spending a week or more of winter deep in the Sierra Nevada, California's magnificent mountain range, had been secretly germinating in the back of my mind for several years.

I had managed to get in a lot of winter mountaineering trips in the Sierra over the past six years, but these consisted primarily of outings of from three to five days. Most of them were done on the east side of the range because of the relatively close access to the high peaks.

Several rewarding climbs had resulted: the first winter ascent of the east ridge of 13,977-foot Mt. Keith, a four-day outing over New Year's Day of 1971; the first winter ascent of 13,570-foot Mt. Brewer, a five-day push six weeks later; in 1970, the second winter ascent of 14,018-foot Mt. Tyndall, on which one of our party fell 800 feet down the peak's north face and had to be rescued by helicopter; and the first winter ascent of the east ridge of 13,986-foot Mt. Humphreys, in 1971.

All these climbs from the eastern approach were tough, brutal endeavors because they involved great and rapid elevation gain, starting as low as 5700 feet at the desert roadhead in the case of Tyndall and Keith, and going up 7000 to 8000 feet in 10 or 12 miles.

Once I managed to get in a particularly exciting winter climb coming in from the west. That was over New Year's in 1969 when Lowell Smith, Eric Adelberger and I probed deep into the range on a 5¼-day outing climaxed by the first winter ascent of Black Kaweah, a towering dark peak of 13,765 feet that had been one of the Sierra's most elusive summits in winter.

Snowshoeing was our mode of travel on all these climbs, although occasionally one or another of our party used cross-country skis. None of us really felt that adept on skis; we were much more comfortable and secure on old-fashioned snowshoes. This was especially true when it came to negotiating steep slopes while carrying 50 to 60 pounds on our backs. Snowshoeing often is slower and more tedious than skiing but it does permit one to get through some kinds of terrain that only the most expert skiers would attempt.

It was in January of this year, just after the holidays, that I began to feel

Self-timer photo (l-r) of Paul Emerson, Carl Smith, Margaret Young on last day of trip.

that familiar winter lure of the Sierra. But I wasn't sure where to go this time, with whom to go, or how many days I could get free. At about the same time, one of my long-time climbing colleagues, Carl Smith, and his friend and fellow-climber, Ted Liston, were hatching a marvelous idea of their own for a winter trek. They wanted to try snowshoeing from one side of the Sierra to the other, and across the very rugged southern part of the range.

The Sierra has been traversed many times in winter, usually in the northern section where the terrain is gentler and the passes relatively easier. But in the south, a region of great, thrusting peaks and steep-walled canyons, such crossings have been extremely rare. Ted and Carl were hoping to make the 50-mile traverse in about 10 days.

All three of us had once spent three memorable weeks in the winter of 1972 climbing in Ecuador, an expedition highlighted by the first repeat of Edware Whymper's first ascent route (southwest ridge) on Chimborazo, in 1880. Retracing the footsteps of this legendary pioneer of mountaineering to the summit of this fabulous 20,561-foot citadel of snow, ice and rock had formed us in a tight bond of friendship.

So, I guess it was only natural that they would invite me to join them on their projected winter adventure. I enthusiastically accepted. Not only would the trip provide a splendid opportunity to climb together again, but also it was a perfect chance, at last, to realize my long-held dream of spending an extended time in the Sierra in the middle of winter.

To bring the team to four members—the size we felt best suited for this type of terrain—we invited Margaret Young to come along. She, too, quickly accepted. Not only was Margaret an old friend and frequent climbing companion on Sierra trips, but she probably brought to our little team more mountaineering experience than the rest of us put together, At one time, Margaret held the American women's altitude record (24,500 feet on Noshaq in the Hindu Kush), and she was a member of the team that made the first all-women's ascent of Mt. McKinley in July of 1970.

Her exploits on mountains throughout the world (Ecuador, Caucusus, Africa, Asia, Alaska, Mexico, Canada and all over the Sierra) have made her just about the top US woman climber today. (Incidentally, she was the member of our team who fell down the face of Mt. Tyndall in 1970 and had to be rescued by helicopter. Miraculously, she lived to tell about it, sustaining only painful bruises and cuts. Three weeks later she was climbing again and that summer went on the McKinley expedition.)

Our trans-Sierra winter traverse took very little advance planning, actually. It was basically all worked out in a few hours at Margaret's house one night as we huddled over maps, charts and aerial photos trying to decide on the most feasible route.

As far as we knew, there had been one previous crossing in winter through this same general area of the Sierra. That was a ski trek in 1952 by a young University of California (Berkeley) student named Allen Steck and three of his friends. They left from Giant Forest on the west side, skied in on the High Sierra Trail, got over Kaweah Gap, proceeded down to the Kern River, then north along the river to Junction Meadow. From there they went due east toward Shepherd Pass and out to the desert. Along the way they made the first ascent of Mt. Tyndall—a fact we were to learn much to our surprise and dismay 18 years later when we made our winter climb of that peak, and read Steck's long-ago note in the summit register.

(Steck, of course, went on to become one of this country's leading mountaineers. In fact, he was on this past summer's American expedition to Mt. Lenin in Russia, and he was among those who discovered the bodies of seven Soviet women climbers who had died the night before in a horrendous storm near Lenin's 24,000-foot summit.)

Our route across the Sierra was in the same general region as Steck's 1952 expedition. But we chose a different way. Our best chances of making it in the 10 days we had allotted ourselves would be to start at the Wolverton roadhead (6700 feet in Giant Forest, not far from Steck's jumping-off point), follow the trail to Pear Lake Hut at 9400 feet, work our way up onto the Tableland and stay as high as possible until getting over what we were sure would be the crux of the entire trip—the 12,200-foot pass on the shoulder of Triple Divide Peak. This we figured would be the point of no return. If we could get over that and safely down into the Kern-Kaweah gorge on the other side, we could snowshoe down to Junction Meadow at 8000 feet, push up along Wallace Creek on the opposite side, cross through the Wright Lakes Basin at 11,500 feet, go over an unnamed pass at 12,000, down and back up again to Shepherd Pass, and then travel the nine twisting miles out to the roadhead at Symmes Creek on the desert floor.

On Friday night, Feb. 22, we crammed ourselves and all our equipment into Margaret's Land Rover in Palo Alto and began the long drive to Wolverton. Plans called for camping at the roadhead that night and getting an early start on snow the next morning.

But when the sun came up we were in a motel in the small farming community of Los Banos, only a third of the way there. The vehicle's left front brake had jammed and forced us to remain overnight until a garage opened. It wasn't until noon that we escaped Los Banos and again were rolling toward the mountains.

By late afternoon we were at Wolverton, sorting and packing all our gear, fuel and food which we had spread all over the pavement of a parking lot. At 5:30 p.m. our trek finally began. Even though it was very late in the day, we were anxious to get going, stretch our legs and start getting used to the heavy loads. Darkness forced a halt at 7 p.m., but by then we already had pushed in three miles. Because the snow on the trail was packed from many previous users going to the hut on the trail, we didn't have to use our snowshoes those first few miles.

Ted had been feeling sub-par all week due to a cold and during the night it got much worse. In the morning he decided to turn back rather than run the risk of getting seriously ill or jeopardizing the expedition. Reluctantly, we agreed his decision was the right one. Being reduced unexpectedly to a three-member party now meant that our packs got a lot heavier all of a sudden as we divided up Ted's share of the group equipment and food, and even some of his personal things we thought we might need.

With a twinge of sadness we waved goodbye to Ted as he started snow-shoeing back down the long slope and out toward the vehicle. The change in plans was discouraging but at least it solved what had been a major logistical problem: assuming we did make it across the Sierra, how were we going to re-trieve Margaret's Land Rover? Ted's illness took care of that.

That day while we slowly sweated our way through and up heavily for-ested slopes, Ted was enjoying a long and leisurely drive home. And probably just about the time he was sitting down to a nice meal at home with his wife and two children, we were stretching out in our sleeping bags inside the tent, trying to adjust to the hard bumps and holes that had formed under our sleep-ing bags. Our camp was pitched at about 10,000 feet in the last clump of trees on the approach to the Tableland.

It had been a strenuous day of snowshoeing, but we still managed to put six miles behind us. The going in mid-afternoon was slowed considerably by the constant clogging of wet snow to the bottom of our snowshoes. Every 100 feet or so we were forced to stop and knock the snow off.

That evening in the tent we leisurely worked our way through a delicious multi-course meal, starting with a drink of piping hot lime jello, followed by soup, the main course of tuna and noodles and cheese, jello instant pudding, cookies and hot chocolate.

Sleep came fitfully and in short stretches that night because our bodies still had not sufficiently adjutsted to the rigorous work, nor were we fully ac-climatized. We were awake at 6 a.m. but it was nearly 8:30 before we got un-derway. Breakfasting and breaking camp each day is a drawn-out affair be-

Paul Emerson photo

Margaret Young starts down a steep, snow-filled ridge after the party had snowshoed over Peak 11,598 on the second day.

cause it involves melting snow for the day's water supply, taking down the tent and repacking all the gear.

It was later on that day that I began to get a sense of the tremendous isolation that's one of the special joys of winter mountaineering. The tremendous expanse of the gently rolling Tableland—a broad plateau covered deeply with beautiful, fresh snow that glistened pristinely under the bright sunshine—accentuated the growing feeling of isolation. In the distance all around us were great peaks and pinnacles. For that brief time, at least, it was great to know we had it all to ourselves.

By noon we had pushed to the end of the Tableland at 11,500 feet, bringing us to a spectacular precipice which afforded sweeping views of the Great Western Divide and the famous Kaweah peaks far ahead, and right below us a group of ice-bound lakes. We also got a good look at the general path of our route for the next two days. From that vantage point it looked even more formidable than we had anticipated.

We snowshoed up and over Peak 11,598 (probably the first time that's ever been done on that peak), headed down to a saddle on the other side and stopped for lunch on several big flat rocks jutting out of the snow. (Lunch time on winter treks is usually determined more by the availability of something nice and dry to sit on than by what hour it is.)

Just beyond the peak was an awesome gash in the ridge, as if someone had taken a giant cleaver and hewn out a 200-foot wide slice in the solid rock. In summer this might have been very hard to cross, but as we have learned through years of snow trekking, travelling in winter is often easier. When else can you go right across the middle of a lake or over small trees, dense brush and giant boulders?

Since this steep-sided chasm was chocked with snow, we dropped straight down one side (now with our snowshoes lashed to our packs), plunging in deeply with every step, and then kicking steps straight up the opposite side. The last 100 feet turned into some rather tricky mixed snow and rock climbing, which Carl expertly led. Trying to do it with a 65-pound pack and four-foot snowshoes attached didn't make it any easier. From the top, Carl leaned down and offered a ski pole for assistance and balance—a nice assist just when hand holds were getting very hard to find.

Once past that obstacle we made good time down a broad ridge, across a long snowfield dotted with rocks and stubby trees, and past a small unnamed lake at 10,800 feet which was covered with snow.

Even though it was past 4 p.m. and the sun was beginning to drop rapidly, we decided to keep pushing on to a col, or saddle, at about 11,4000 feet in an effort to get at least one more big hurdle behind us. Two vigorous hours of snowshoeing, much of it on very hard, steep snow which we negotiated only with the help of our trusty ski poles, brought us up to the col. We dropped over the other side into the huge cirque which runs along under Elizabeth Pass and extends for several miles across and around to Coppermine Peak, which was to be the next day's first major barrier.

About one-quarter mile out onto the cirque we found a spot level enough for a tent site. With darkness moving in and the temperature dropping noticeably, we laboriously stomped out with our snowshoes a platform for the tent on the soft, deep snow. Whenever we tried to moved around within the shoes, we found ourselves plunging in up to our hips or waist.

Cooking is slow and tedious in winter and requires great care lest the stove or pots of water get accidentally tipped over inside the tent. Yet, the cooking and eating helps pass the hours when there's nothing else to do. Once the stove gets going it radiates a comforting kind of emotional warmth right along with the amazing amount of heat it generates under the cooking pots.

To make the task of melting snow easier, we filled a large plastic bag—one of those used as garbage can liners—with clean snow every night and brought it inside the tent. That way we would have a sufficient supply for both dinner and the next day's breakfast without ever having to go back outside or open the tent door every so often to scoop up more snow, thereby letting a lot of cold air rush in.

A typical meal on a winter trip like this takes about two hours from beginning to end. But it's very important to keep oneself supplied with plenty of good food to keep the energy level high and to withstand prolonged exposure to the elements.

Margaret Young crossing the saddle (elev. 11,400) of "El Cap Pass."

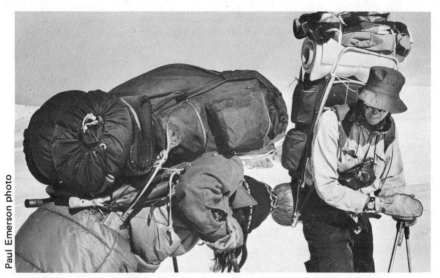

Paul Emerson photo

Carl Smith and Margaret Young (left, leaning on her ski poles)
during a brief rest stop.

When the sun hit our camp the next morning we stepped outside to be
greeted by a fabulous sight. The rock spire above us and the peak just to our
right took on an entirely different look than they had the night before. In
the early sunlight, they had a fiery, reddish coloration that was sharply
accentuated by the dark azure sky beyond. Since the peak on the right so
closely resembled a miniature El Capitan, we decided, for easy reference, to
name the saddle we had come over the night before "El Cap Pass."

On Tuesday, our third full day out, the weather continued warm and
sunny as we plowed through deep snow at about the 11,000-foot contour
under Elizabeth Pass and on toward Coppermine Peak (12,340 ft.). To reach
the saddle below the peak took great effort, but by making large switchbacks,
we were able to snowshoe to within 100 feet. At this point the snow became
too hard and steep for snowshoes. So, we removed them and kicked steps
straight up to the saddle. After a short rest, we put on crampons and tight-
rope walked our way up the narrow snow ridge to the top of Coppermine
Peak and dropped down another ridge leading off to the east. A couple of
hours of tough snowshoing, cramponing and even scrambling on all fours at
one point finally brought us to Glacier Lake at 11,600 ft.

It was 3 p.m. and overcast, and we had to decide whether to camp there
or push on over Triple Divide Peak Pass--now only a steep mile ahead. Anxious
to get that barrier behind us, we pushed on, alternating the lead to make the
laborious job of breaking trail less demanding. The difficulties of the pass
were foremost in our mind, but a couple of unexpected surprises made the rest
of that day much more than we had ever bargained for.

We all were rounding into top shape. Legs and lungs were responding
well to the demands and our stamina and staying power were building well.

Even though the sky was clouding up fast and the hint of a snowstorm was in the air, we kept pushing hard. The final drive to the pass itself required crampons all the way because of the almost ice-like consistency of the snow and the steep angle of the slope.

The straight up route brought us quickly to the top of the 12,200-foot pass, where we were greeted by a cutting, cold wind whipping up strongly from the other side. The sharp dip in the temperature sent us all scurrying to our packs in search of more clothing.

In planning this expedition the only peak we were allowing ourselves to climb was a possible attempt on 12,634-foot Triple Divide itself. Although not exceptionally high by Sierra standards, it is nonetheless an important landmark in the range because it stands at the head of three major watersheds. From the pass the summit loomed up invitingly only a third of a mile away at the end of a jagged and corniced ridge. We circled up and over to the summit ridge, dropped our packs and rope on the rocks and set out for the top.

The farther out we got, the narrower and steeper and more exposed the ridge became. After awhile it was difficult to tell when we were on solid

Snowshoeing across a huge cirque at about 11,000 feet en route to Coppermine Peak.

Paul Emerson photo

snow or treading precariously out on an overhanging cornice. The summit was about 100 feet above us and 100 yards or so away when, with Carl in the lead, we suddenly heard a crunching, cracking sound. The snow under Carl's feet gave way. Instantly, he lunged to his right and scrambled safely onto solid snow while the chunk of cornice he had inadvertently trod on, went plummeting straight down more than 1000 feet into the Kern-Kaweah gorge below.

We had come within an eyelash of disaster, and seeing that the remaining part of the ridge above was even more hazardous, we decided to beat a hasty retreat. Had we been roped up along that ridge, there probably would have been no serious risks, but we weren't roped up. Why we had left the rope behind still puzzles us to this day. Perhaps we underestimated the ridge's difficulties or the long, tough day of climbing had made us so weary we lacked the alertness to make sound judgments.

As Carl and I started back down the ridge to our packs, Margaret tarried awhile to inspect the fracture line in the cornice. Just then another large section snapped off inches from the toes of her boots. Half a foot more and she would have gone a 1000 feet down. That was all the prodding she needed to quickly catch up with us.

Back at the packs Carl, now much more relaxed, joked about the near miss and said, "Well, I guess we've had our excitement for the day." But he was wrong. Another frightening experience was just ahead.

While cramponing down the 2,000-foot slope into the Kern-Kaweah gorge, we found ourselves suddenly hung up in a huge band of rocks about two-thirds of the way down. The weight of our packs and snowshoes made it difficult braking against the downward pull, especially on the extremely hard snow. By now it was after 6 p.m., darkness was closing in rapidly, and there was still 800 feet to go. Mentally I began preparing myself for the unpleasant possibliity of spending the night bivouacked up there out in the open clinging to some rock.

We were fairly well spread out, each of us trying to find our own way through. Sometimes we'd find a promising route only to be led into something even steeper and more exposed. Slowly and carefully, we zig-zagged from rock to rock, using our ice axes to control the descent. Since my long snowshoes were constantly getting hung up on the slope and threatening to throw me off balance, I decided to get rid of them and sent them skimming down to the bottom of the canyon.

That helped considerably and after 15 more minutes of tense down-climbing, I finally got through the rock band and onto better snow. Carl and Margaret, who had just come out down below, were a bit startled to see one of my snowshoes go careening by. For a time, since I was out of sight and ear-shot, they thought I might have had an accident.

At 10 minutes after 7 p.m. we staggered onto a spot near the floor of the gorge that was flat enough for a tent. After 11 consecutive hours of arduous snowshoeing and climbing, we barely had enough energy left to get the tent up and crawl inside, almost totally exhausted. We settled for a skimpy dinner of soup and hot lemonade and turned in for the night.

Next morning we awoke to overcast skis and the sounds of a light snowfall. The snowshoeing was mostly downhill that day as we headed for our next destination, Junction Meadow. Moisture and heat from the river flowing under the snow created big icy hummocks which, although very picturesque, were tricky to snowshoe through and around. We munched a cold lunch in the gently falling snow at Gallats Lake around noon, and after a lot of up-and-down travelling to get past the steep walls alongside Rockslide Lake, we eventually came into the flat, heavily forested confines of Junction Meadow.

Two coyotes standing alertly on a patch of snow eyed us with surprise and suspicion as we trudged the last few hundred yards to the meadow. As we drew closer, they bolted uphill and disappeared in some trees. Their surprise was understandable, since most likely we were the first people to come through this area at that time of the year since Steck and his party skied through there in the winter of 1952.

We were at 8,000 feet, the low point of the trip, elevation-wise, but, psychologically, one of the high points. In four rugged days we had snowshoed halfway across the Sierra, putting the most difficult terrain behind us.

Now, it would be just a matter of working our way up 4,000 feet of gentler slopes on the other side, getting over Shepherd Pass and then dropping

Paul Emerson having lunch in the snow after crossing Coppermine Peak.

down and out to the desert. We guessed wrong again. The snowshoeing may have been easier, the packs lighter, our bodies in terrific shape, but by the time we were to escape the mountains four days later, it almost got down to a matter of survival.

The easy availability of running water from the fast-moving Kaweah River just a few yards from our tent made Junction Meadow one of the most pleasant camp sites of the entire trip. Except for the sound of rushing water, the valley was exceptionally quiet and peaceful when we awoke the next morning. Our isolation from civilization seemed more pronounced than ever, and the heavy stillness hanging over the meadow allowed us to savor every moment.

When we started up the opposite side toward Wallace Creek, we could look far down the Kern Canyon to the south and see a big storm brewing up and closing in fast. By lunchtime it was snowing heavily and we were forced to stand under a large, lightning-ravaged tree to get what limited shelter we could find. We pushed on again after only 10 minutes. Deep snow and poor visibility brought us to an early halt that day around 4 p.m., and we set up camp in a densely wooded area at about 10,300 feet.

So much new snow fell during the night that it piled up all night around the tent, caving in the sides and cutting in half our usable space inside. Our sleeping bags and clothes were fairly wet by morning, and as usual, our boots frozen stiff.

Perhaps we should have stayed there in the protection of the woods to ride out the storm, but with time getting short we decided to move on. A tough slog straight up the steep hill above us took us out onto the Wright Lakes Basin and into a virtual white-out.

Carl's skillful use of the compass, however, steered an amazingly true course through this blind, wide-open plateau. About the only thing we could see were a few rocks and trees poking up out of the snow. We used these as short-term goals to relieve the monotony of this seemingly endless march through "nothingness."

A strong wind developed as we gained altitude, and after we got over one ridge, it began to buffet us unmercifully. It was all we could do to stand up against it, and occasionally extra strong gusts knocked us to our knees like a half-dazed boxer. The wind and white-out forced us to give up at mid-afternoon, and there out in the middle of that unprotected plateau, we tried to put up the tent. I crawled inside and stood for 20 minutes struggling to hold the center pole upright, while Margaret and Carl worked their way around outside, anchoring the tent down with ski poles, ice axes and snowshoes. They even used the climbing rope to tie the tent to a big boulder nearby as insurance in case the tent blew down.

Once inside we got the stove going immediately and thawed ourselves out with a brew of hot jello drink, to which we added the last few drops of Ted's brandy. All night long the wind hammered us ferociously; occasionally, the wind would die down for a few seconds, only to erupt again with explosive force. We lay there watching the sides of the tent sway, sag, and snap under the pounding force of what must have been winds approaching 80 mph., thinking that any moment the tent would be ripped apart. Margaret was less worried;

after all, she had ridden out a six-day storm on McKinley in this same tent.

During the night, however, one of the ropes outside snapped and caused the tent to pitch over at about 45 degrees. A small opening was forced in one of the doors and an inch or two of spindrift snow was blasted through, covering our bags, stove, pots, food and even our faces as we slept.

We remained in the tent for several hours the next morning to clean up the mess and discuss the pros and cons of moving on. The weather conditions remained unchanged, and even seemed worse. Also very much on our minds were the whereabouts of John Emerson, my brother. He also is an avid winter mountaineer, but with a penchant for going solo—even though this violates every rule in the book. He knew of our trans-Sierra crossing and appproximately when and where we were expected to emerge on the east side. John decided to make a solo outing of his own to coincide with ours, going up Shepherd Pass from the east. He wanted to climb Mt. Young, then meet us on the way out and go down to the desert with us. But we had no idea if he went through with his plans, and if so, how he was faring in this storm.

Inactivity and curiosity got the better of us around noon, and we decided to break camp and start groping toward the 12,000 foot unnamed pass that would put us on target for Shepherd. Through the white-out it began to emerge, at first just a few high rocks, then later giant slopes of rock and snow looming out of the whiteness like ghostly spectres.

I was the first to reach the pass, and as I snowshoed through, the sight of a bright red ribbon caught my eye. It was wrapped around a cairn of rocks and I knew immediately it must be a sign from my brother. It was! Hidden in the cairn was a plastic butter container with a hastily scribbled note from John. He told of being caught there in the storm, and after settling for a climb of nearby Tawny Point, decide to retreat. He wished us well and hoped we would make it through okay.

As we were to find out later, John returned to Shepherd Pass but because of the white-out found it unsafe to descend. So, he put up his tent there at 12,000 feet and for three nights remained pinned down in the storm.

On the evening of the third day there, about 1 o'clock in the morning, John's tent blew down. He crawled outside in the darkness and icy wind and spent nearly half an hour before getting the tent upright again. Under those horrible conditions he was able to make only tenuous supports at best, so when he got back inside he had to spend the rest of the night clutching tight-ly to the pole to make sure the tent didn't blow down again.

What he hadn't noticed at first was that during those terrible moments outside, the wind had blown snow in through the bottoms of his gloves. By the time he got back inside and could remove the gloves, his wrists and finger-tips had been frostbitten.

Early the next morning, realizing he had to get down or run the risk of dying up there of exposure should his tent blow down again, John decided to descend the pass, even though the white-out was as bad as ever. It was a harrow-ing downclimb and the wind was so fierce it nearly toppled him on several occasions, but somehow he made it safely to the bottom and out of the worst of the wind.

Paul Emerson photo

The first night of the storm more than two feet of snow fell, "caving in the sides of the tent and cutting in half our usable space inside."

That same night we were still caught up in the full fury of the storm and beginning to seriously wonder if we'd ever get out. There was no sign of a let-up. To stay warm that night we resorted to filling our plastic water bottles with boiling water and using them as old-fashioned water bottles inside our sleeping bags. They worked beautifully and retained their heat for hours.

We need that extra warmth. The night was long and bitterly cold. The air from our breathing formed a thin layer of snow crystals on the inside walls of the tent, but the wind kept continually shaking them loose and causing a miniature snowfall inside. Our sleeping bags were very damp in the morning and the exteriors were frozen stiff.

However, we were too preoccupied to notice. Our attention was diverted by something much more delightful: the sun was out and the wind seemed to be dying. When we finally broke camp, Sunday, March 3, the sky had cleared and we were treated to magnificent vistas of the Great Western Divide and the Kaweahs—four days by snowshoes behind us—and a whole host of other great Sierra peaks, all dazzling and resplendent in their fresh blanket of snow.

As we snowshoed past Mt Tyndall on our right a little later, we got a great look at the steep north face where Margaret had taken her wild ride down four winters before. At Shepherd Pass I discovered another note from my brother (actually written a day before the other one) and Carl uncovered a large stuff sack half-buried in the snow which contained a lot of my brother's marginal food and gear. It was the first indication I had that he had been in serious trouble.

The drop straight down the deep snow in the pass was glorious, except for a few tentative moments skirting under several large cornices that appeared ready to avalanche at any moment. Fresh avalanche debris was in evidence all over the run-out of the slope below us. Once off the pass we got back on our snowshoes and started downhill. By mid-afternoon we caught up to my brother's snowshoe tracks. Unfortunately for him but lucky for us, he already had done miles of trail-breaking in the nearly three feet of fresh powder.

Then, about 4 o'clock, I turned a sharp bend in the trail and there, 200 yards ahead, battling through the deep snow, was my brother John. I shouted excitedly and he looked around, a bit startled at first. Then he let out a loud whoop and a holler. Within minutes we all were enjoying a grand Sierra rendezvous, at 9,000 feet and four miles from trail's end. John and I toasted each other with a Wyler's raspberry drink while Carl recorded the moment on film.

Later, on the way out, John showed me the ugly frostbite blisters that had developed on his fingertips and wrists and related the events of those grim nights alone in the storm.

We all had been over this terrain of the Shepherd Pass Trail many times in winter, but never before was the trip out so delightful. One nice thing awaiting us at the road was my brother's car, which meant that we wouldn't have to trudge five or six miles across the desert in the dark to reach civilization at Independence.

It was nearly dark when we arrived at the car, and even though the vehicle had been sitting there for five days in frigid weather, it started right up. We then drove to nearby Lone Pine to celebrate with a steak dinner at the fanciest restaurant in town. The three of us men, with our heavy beards and bright red, windburned faces and dirty clothes, were out of place, but no one in the restaurant seemed to care. Margaret only had to run a comb through her hair a few times and she looked as pretty as ever.

That night we stayed over in a local motel, and after breakfast the next morning, John drove us to the Lone Pine Airport where Margaret's plane was waiting to take us home. Friends of hers had flown the plane over for her a week earlier. John, meanwhile, went to the hospital to have his frostbite treated before starting the long drive alone back to the San Francisco Bay Area.

On the flight back to Palo Alto, Margaret flew over the exact route of our 50-mile sojourn on snow. Each spot along our route brought a flood of memories of the adventure rushing through our minds. The scene of our near-disaster on that snowy ridge of Triple Divide Peak looked even more frightening from the air.

What took us nine rigorous but exciting days to cover on the ground, took only 40 minutes by air. Our snowshoe tracks coming down Shepherd Pass were still clearly visible, but beyond that the wind and snow had completely obliterated any trace that we had ever been there.

The Only One

Nordic World, the cross-country skier's magazine, is the first and only magazine offering complete year-round coverage of the entire nordic sports scene: ski touring, snow camping, ski jumping, dog sledding, ski mountaineering—all those great winter sports which have been overlooked by the media for so long.

Nordic World has become the center for nordic enthusiasm, as the leading figures in the sport are contributing outstanding articles and photos to help every nordic skier—beginner or expert—enjoy their sport to the fullest. For the technique, training, touring, equipment and personal experience articles, subscribe to **Nordic World** magazine.

WINTER CAMPING BOOKLIST

If you'd like to read more about winter camping, we recommend the following books. You may find them at your local bookstore, but you'll probably have better luck ordering directly from World Publications, Box 366, Mountain View, CA 94040.

Winter Hiking and Camping, John Danielson. An Adirondack Mountain Club book written primarily for winter campers and hikers in the New England states. Offers sound advice for all, and is especially good for its chapters on dealing with the effects of cold on yourself and your equipment. 1972 hardback, 192 pp., ill., $4.95.

Paradise Below Zero, Calvin Rutstrum. Best-selling handbook on how to camp in winter, by one of America's foremost wilderness writers. Covers every way to get around in winter—from snowshoes to sled dogs—and every way you can make yourself safe and comfortable while snow camping. 1968 paperback, 256 pp., ill., $2.45.

The Complete Snow Camper's Guide, Raymond Bridge. The emphasis is on safety—the real needs of the winter camper and how he or she can best meet them. Contains excellent equipment sections and a much-needed plea for the retention of the natural beauty of the winter landscape. 1973 paperback, 396 pp., ill., $5.95.

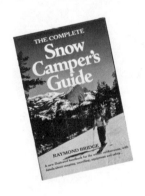

Frostbite, Bradford Washburn. A useful little book which scientifically and at the same time practically tells what happens when frostbite occurs, and how to prevent it. Really a vital book for the winter sports enthusiast. 1973 paperback, 30 pp., ill., $1.50.

The Cross-Country Ski, Cook, Look, and Pleasure Book, Hal Painter. A really new and different approach to winter sports. This book manages to be useful (although we wouldn't recommend it for your *only* reference source), but is always amusing. It might be X-rated by some, but will be enjoyed by all. 1973 paperback, 168 pp., ill., $4.95.

World Publications   Box 366, Mountain View, CA 94040